31|10|16

T

D0808833

BRENT LIBRARIES

91120000197413

Other books by Guy Claxton:
Hare Brain, Tortoise Mind: Why Intelligence Increases When You Think Less
Wise Up: Learning to Live the Learning Life
Building Learning Power
The Wayward Mind: an intimate history of the unconscious

Other books by Bill Lucas:
Power Up Your Mind: Learn Faster, Work Smarter
Help Your Child to Succeed (with Alistair Smith)
Happy Families: how to make one, how to keep one
Boost Your Mind Power Week by Week

The Creative Thinking Plan

HOW TO GENERATE IDEAS AND SOLVE PROBLEMS IN YOUR WORK AND LIFE

GUY CLAXTON AND BILL LUCAS

BBC ACTIVE

With thanks to Henrietta Lucas, for patiently reading the
manuscript and making lots of helpful improvements, and
to Judith Nesbitt, for support and encouragement.

Published by BBC Books, BBC Worldwide Limited,
Woodlands, 80 Wood Lane, London W12 0TT

First published under the title *Be Creative* in 2004.
This revised edition published in 2007

8   7   6   5   4

ISBN 978-1-4066-1425-1

Commissioning Editor: Emma Shackleton
Project Editor: Jeanette Payne
Designer: Kevin O'Connor
Picture Researcher: Rachel Jordan
Production Controller: Man Fai Lau

Set in Frutiger
Printed and bound in Malaysia (CTP-VVP)

Contents

Learn to embrace uncertainty and unleash your creativity

How to use *The Creative Thinking Plan*

This book is for people who want to tap into their creative roots, who want to know how to induce the state of mind in which good ideas flow more freely and who are interested in trying out some exercises that will help them achieve those goals for themselves.

For many of the exercises, you will find it helpful to have the CD version of this book, which is called *Be Creative*, or to make audio recordings of the key parts.

Introduction: the four ways of creativity

In his famous book *The Little Prince*, Antoine de Saint-Exupéry records this conversation between the prince, who has just arrived on a new planet, and the first person he meets, the lamplighter.

> 'Good morning. Why have you just put out your lamp?'
>
> 'These are the instructions,' replied the lamplighter. 'Good morning.'
>
> 'What are the instructions?'
>
> 'The instructions are that I put out my lamp. Good evening.' And he lighted his lamp again.
>
> 'But why have you just lighted it again?'
>
> 'These are the instructions,' replied the lamplighter.
>
> 'I don't understand,' said the little prince.
>
> 'There is nothing to understand,' said the lamplighter. 'Instructions are instructions. Good morning.' And he put out his lamp.
>
> Then he mopped his forehead with a handkerchief decorated with red squares. 'I follow a terrible profession. In the old days it was reasonable. I put the lamp out in the morning and in the evening I lighted it again. I had the rest of the day for relaxation and the rest of the night for sleep.'
>
> 'And the instructions have been changed since that time?'
>
> 'The instructions have not been changed,' said the lamplighter. 'That is the tragedy! From year to year the planet has turned more rapidly and the orders have *not* been changed.'

What it takes to get on in life depends on the kind of world you inhabit. We need to be smart, creative and flexible according to the circumstances in which we find ourselves. And as those change, so we need to respond in different ways. There was a time when the lamplighter's ability to follow instructions meticulously and responsibly was smart. But not any longer. Now that kind of smart has effectively become dumb. What he needs now is not loyalty but creativity.

To be smart today means being able to come up with fresh ideas whenever you need them. Creativity is no longer something we can admire in an Einstein or a Mozart, while we plod along, lighting our lamps and putting them out. Our world has changed dramatically. Artists, musicians and the best scientists have always needed to be creative: to use their initiative, take risks and ask good questions. Now, so do solo parents, financial advisers, skateboarders, middle managers, the expanding numbers of self-employed people – all of us.

There has never been more uncertainty than there is in today's fast-moving world. Even as we solve one mystery – such as the decoding of DNA – we discover another, such as the impact of genetically modified foods. The lamplighter would not have known what to do in today's world; he might not even have recognized the fact that no new instructions would be forthcoming.

According to thinkers like Alvin Toffler, a 'totally new social force, a stream of change so accelerated that it influences our sense of time' has been unleashed upon us. The tempo of daily life is such that everything looks and feels different. Consider these statements:

It is not possible to fly to Barcelona for less than the price of a second-class train ticket between London and Winchester.

Civil aeroplanes could not possibly be used as missiles.

Universities are only for the clever few.

A young English writer could not possibly amass more wealth in a few years than the current queen of England's family has saved over many centuries.

Individual terrorists cannot be as dangerous as rogue states.

How can an easyJet plane ride be cheaper than the train? How is it possible that an unemployed single mother called J.K. Rowling could become a global publishing phenomenon? Nothing is predictable anymore. And things that seem simple are actually complex. When Francis Bacon wrote: 'If a man shall begin with certainties, he shall end in doubts; but if he will be content to begin with doubts, he shall end in certainties', he might have been thinking about our complex contemporary society. If we are to survive, let alone thrive in this world, we have to find ways of living with the uncertainties that it brings, and crafting for ourselves new solutions to both old and new problems: how to relate to adolescents seemingly from another planet; how to make a living; how to use our leisure, and so on.

A new view of creative thought

The new world brings with it a new view of creativity. We now know that creativity is something we all have. It's neither a gift given to the lucky few nor a skill we can fake with a few tricks. Everyone can learn to be more creative. We're never going to be as fast or strong as Ashia Hansen or Steve Redgrave, but that doesn't mean it's a waste of time going to the gym – far from it. And just because we are (probably) not going to be the next Madonna or Versace, it doesn't mean we can't get better at thinking creatively.

Our aim is to convince you that it is possible to gently cultivate your mind so that it naturally grows more good ideas – and to show you how to do it. This approach works simultaneously in four different ways:

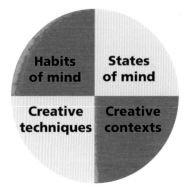

Practise these, and you will slowly but surely come to be more creative, in all areas of your life. (Take a look at the diagram of contents on pages 20 and 120.)

■ The first way: Habits of mind

The latest psychology shows that your mental temperament and attitudes are not set in stone. You learnt them as you were growing up, and you can change them now. Personality is as much a matter of habit as it is of God- or gene-given predispositions and limitations. If you want to, you can build up your mental 'physique', just as you can develop your fitness or stamina. You can practise being more persistent in the face of difficulty. You can learn to handle complexity and confusion better. You can build up your patience. You can learn to take different perspectives, and see other people's point of view. You can become better at asking and refining questions. You can protect your intrinsic interest, and learn how to be creative for both love and money. All of these habits contribute to developing more creative minds. We will teach you some exercises that will strengthen the attitudes you need to support your creativity.

The second way: States of mind

Everybody knows that the quality of their attention or the sharpness of their wits varies a good deal. Sometimes you are really on the ball; sometimes a bit more muzzy or foggy. What people are less aware of is that they are more able to control their states of mind than th̲ ̲ ̲ ̲ ̲ ̲ ̲ ̲ ̲ ̲ ̲ ̲ ̲ ̲ ̲fferent states of mind are good for different kinds of t̲ ̲ ̲ ̲ ̲ ̲ ̲ ̲ ̲ ̲ ̲ ̲ ̲d to be funny when you are uptight. It is hard to co̲ ̲ ̲ ̲ ̲ ̲ ̲ate on f̲ ̲ ̲ ̲etail when you are tired. One of the new keys to creativity is the realization that *the ability to move flexibly and appropriately between different dimensions of awareness is vital*.

In the course of a day, you can shuttle between many different states of mind. Sometimes thoughts and sensations chase themselves quickly across the screen of consciousness. Sometimes they move slowly and sluggishly. Sometimes there is a strong sense of being in control of the mind's activity. And sometimes it feels as if this activity is going on all by itself, as though you are more of an observer of your mind than an active director or participant.

Three *dimensions* particularly affect your state of mind: focus, orientation and sociability. (Again, look at the diagram of contents on pages 20 and 120.)

Creative dimensions
Focus

Sometimes the quality of the mind is sharp and purposeful, absorbed in a single experience or a single train of thought, while at others it is more dreamy, playful, diffused and receptive. Let's call this dimension the degree of *focus* of your awareness.

Orientation

Your attention can be turned outwards towards the external world, busy absorbing information, or it can be inward-looking and reflective, mulling over what has already been learned, searching for deeper meaning and new connections. This is the *orientation* dimension of your attention.

Sociability

Often you are sociable, keen to kick ideas around, to immerse yourself in other people's perspectives and ready to put your ideas to public test. And, sometimes, your mood is solitary – you are content puzzling things out for yourself. We call this the *sociability* dimension.

You need to be adept at exploring each aspect of the three dimensions. And you need to be able to toggle between them as and when they are appropriate. Think of it as if you were controlling the console of your own mind with some kind of lever, able to shift fluidly between hard-focused and soft-focused, inward and outward, and solitary and sociable attention. Being creative involves learning to draw more fully and more flexibly on these three dimensions of the mind – and we will show you how to do it.

There is one combination of these dimensions that we'll give most attention to: the one that involves being playfully receptive, inward and solitary. This is often the one that people have most trouble with, and it is the one that is most crucial to the vital process at the heart of creativity: having fresh ideas bubble up into your mind. Having good ideas is the key phase of creative problem-solving. Good ideas emerge in a certain mental mood that can be learnt and cultivated, a special combination of relaxation and alertness. The more you are able to tune in to that mood, the more hospitable your mind becomes to new ideas.

▮ The third way: Creative techniques

Special processes or exercises can stimulate different aspects of the creative process. However – and this is important – particular techniques of creativity are state-of-mind dependent. They work differently depending on the frame of mind you are in. A very focused, busy frame of mind sometimes comes up with hare-brained ideas. But when people are in a more receptive, leisurely mood, the quality of ideas they generate improves. And they do better still if they create time to move between thinking aloud together, and mulling things over on their own.

So when you are able to make more flexible and intelligent use of the three dimensions – focus, orientation and sociability – particular techniques become more powerful. (It's the same as trying to use time-management techniques. When you are totally stressed out, making lists is the last thing you can cope with doing. But after a good game of squash, or a long slow bath, you might be in a much better frame of mind to tackle tidying up your agenda of tasks.)

■ The fourth way: Creative contexts

The fourth and last way of working concerns context. We will show what a positive creative environment is like – we call this *creatogenic* – and, by contrast, what a negative or *creatocidal* one is. How creative you are depends on where you find yourself. Most people are more creative as they are dropping off to sleep than they were in the crucial committee meeting earlier on in the day. And how creative they were in that meeting depends on the way it was run and the atmosphere in the room. One critical, point-scoring, creatocidal individual can make people so defensive that their creativity shrivels up and dies. Even the way the chairs are laid out and how the breaks are managed can make a difference. You may not be able to control much of the situation in which you find yourself, but everybody, once they become aware of it, can find some elbow room to shape a more creatogenic environment – physically as well as socially.

You can even manage your own lifestyle and health so that you are more likely to respond creatively, rather than dogmatically or stereotypically, when the occasion demands it. We shall point out for you some of the areas in which you may have more control than you think over your own creative ecology.

OK, that's the bones of our approach. In the rest of this introduction we want to set the scene a little more before starting in earnest.

■ Your view of the world

'From a worldly point of view, there is no mistake so great as that of being always right.'

Samuel Butler

Consider this paradox. Blowing on a match puts it out. Blowing on an ember makes it burst into life. If the first puff on the match doesn't extinguish it, it is smart to puff harder. If the puff on the ashes rekindles the fire when your intention was to put it out, it is stupid to blow harder. And as the world turns faster and faster, so there comes a point where persisting in all situations with the kind of abstract, logical, deliberate intelligence that has been fashionable for so long becomes counter-productive. You end up being an increasingly forlorn lamplighter.

The same dilemma often faces us when things go wrong. If the car's engine will not start, it may be smart to try to trace the fault logically. But when a relationship gets into trouble, endless analysis, however clever, may not be the answer. Trying to pinpoint exactly where your marriage went wrong may not be helpful. Making the effort to feel what it is like to be your partner might be much more productive. Your reactions will depend on how you see the world.

Here is an exercise, the first of many in this book, which is designed to help you see what kind of world you envisage for yourself and your children and grandchildren.

NOW TRY THIS: What kind of world do you see?

Look through the following list of words and tick those that seem to you to apply to the world as you experience it, or as you imagine today's children, the citizens of 2020 and beyond, will find it.

demanding	safe	uncertain	challenging
predictable	tranquil	risky	secure
calm	unstable	changing	simple
agreed	reliable	sheltered	complicated
disputed	traditional	diverse	fluid

What do these words mean to you? What kinds of mental and emotional qualities do you think people need most in order to be able to thrive in such a world? Do you feel you possess these qualities as much as you would like? Do your children? Does your boss?

If you ticked mostly the 'safe', 'predictable' kinds of words, then you may find that some of the ideas we are advancing in *The Creative Thinking Plan* are particularly challenging. We hope you will enjoy the dialogue with us! If you ticked mostly the other kind, what follows will more obviously fit with your view of the world.

Introducing hard and soft focus

We especially need good ideas when our preconceptions are confounded and our familiar habits don't work. Creative is what you need to be when there is no section in the manual to tell you how to deal with this situation, and your reflex problem-solving responses aren't up to it.

Let's talk a little more about those states of mind in which creative ideas just seem to bubble up: the ones that are more receptive, more relaxed, more inward, more passive, more playful and less controlled. The birth of an idea may be preceded and followed by modes of attention that are much more focused, purposeful and often intellectual. Indeed, without such preparation the ideas may not emerge, and without the follow-up they may not become practical and strong. But if the change of pace and tone is not allowed to occur, then they may not come at all.

It is not hard to see why you need both the hard- and soft-focus modes. Imagine you find yourself in a pitch-black cave with two sources of illumination: a small spotlight with a very bright, very narrow beam, and an old hurricane lamp that sheds a dim, diffuse light. Which would you want to use first in order to get your bearings? The spotlight would not be a great deal of use at this stage. It would pick out small details, but you would have no idea what they were details of, nor how they fitted together. Though it is only dim, the hurricane lamp would give you a much better sense of the lie of the land. It gives you the big picture. Once you have got a feel for the space, *then* you may well want to check out different aspects of it in more detail, and now the focused beam of the spotlight comes into its own.

Now imagine that you are standing at the mouth of the cave, and this variable beam of light can be directed either outwards into the night to see what is out there, or inwards, back into the cave, to check on what resources you have to hand. In just the same way, we can swivel our attention backwards and forwards between the outside world – what was that noise? – and the inner theatre of fantasies and thoughts – back to that daydream of fame and fortune.

Focusing in four dimensions

This simple table describes these four predominant *solitary* dimensions of mind (we will get back to the sociable side of creativity later on). We can look inwards and outwards, and can be hard or soft focus. Because we live in a predominantly hard-focus culture, we need to emphasize the value of the softer ways of seeing and thinking – because, as we have seen, when it comes to creativity, it is the mixture of soft and hard that is smart, and hard-only looks increasingly dumb.

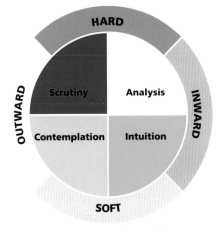

The ability to drop into the state of mind that enables you to sense the world in a contemplative, holistic way, and to draw on your own inner knowledge and experience intuitively, is absolutely of the essence. Being able to tune in to the state of relaxed alertness essential to creative thinking is so important that we are going to invite you to dive straight into a relaxation exercise, designed to remind you of what 'relaxed alertness' feels like.

This kind of exercise will be familiar to people who have attended a yoga class or an antenatal course. It involves taking a long, slow scan through your body, gently seeing what small sensations you find in different locations, without trying to alter them, or think about them. At the end of the exercise, we will invite you to see if your body and your mind feel quieter and more relaxed. If they do, we suggest that you use the most alert corner of the mind to make a mental note of just what this quality of awareness feels like, so that you will form a clear memory that you can retrieve later, to remind you what the relaxed-alert state is like. We suggest that you attach a mental label to this image – a simple word or phrase of your own. This can then act in the future as your password or access code, to get back into this state of mind more quickly.

Once you are comfortable with this exercise, you will have acquired the first of a number of creative techniques that will serve you well in cultivating a creative state of mind.

NOW TRY THIS: How to relax

Use these instructions to guide you as you gently try to place your attention in different parts of your body and consciously feel whatever sensations might be there. It is best to do the exercise with your eyes closed, so either have the *Be Creative* CD playing, or get a friend to read the instructions out to you. (Choose a friend who has a gentle, soothing voice.) Even if you *could* read with your eyes closed, it would be distracting reading out the instructions at the same time as trying to follow them. Many commercially produced tapes that follow a similar pattern are available, but your own would probably be just as good. Make sure that you do it slowly, leaving plenty of spaces in which to follow the instructions and feel your way into your body. As a rough guide, the exercise should take about 15 minutes, so that's how long your recording ought to be.

You will find your mind doing different things each time you try this exercise (and, simple though it is, it really repays repeating at regular intervals). Sometimes you will feel drowsy, no matter what posture you adopt. If that happens a lot, try doing the exercise at a different time of day. Experiment with where you can fit it into your schedule, and at the same time try to find when your mind is most amenable to entering the relaxed-alert state. If you drop off, don't worry; a good sleep is worth having, too. Or, if you can find an awake corner of your mind, use it to watch the drowsy bit. What does 'drowsy' feel like? Where in your body do you experience 'drowsy' most strongly? Try to notice the quality of mind that goes along with 'drowsy' (before you finally fall asleep). And so on.

You can also try the same tactics if you start to feel restless, tense or irritated. See if you can find a relaxed-alert part of the mind that is able to observe – in an alert but relaxed fashion – the nature of the irritation or tension. And then, of course, you are equally free to give up – for the moment.

Another thing that people often experience is the mind wandering off. Instead of being aware of your left knee, you find yourself listening to the sound of the air-conditioning, or remembering the holiday you had on the Isle of Wight when you were seven. By the time you come to, you find that you have got up to the top of your head, but you have missed the whole of your body in between. If this happens, relax. It isn't a problem. It happens to everybody (even Zen masters drift off now and again). Just ask your mind politely if it is ready to leave the alternative attraction and come back to the body scan. If it is, welcome back. If it isn't, don't struggle. Go with whatever is pulling your attention most strongly. (There will be a good reason for it, whether you can see that or not.) So here we go.

- Sit in a comfortable chair, one that encourages you to be fairly upright, with hands resting comfortably in your lap. You could lie down, but this can induce the 'relaxed' without the 'alert' and send you to sleep.
- Find a comfortable but reasonably upright posture and close your eyes. Take a moment to feel your attention turning inwards. Ask yourself: what is it like to be me right at this moment? How does my body feel? Easy? Tense? Tired? Jumpy? What word comes to mind for your general physical state?... Now do the same for your emotional state. How are you feeling right now? Expectant? Suspicious? Happy? What? Find your own word... Now do the same thing for your state of mind. What kind of quality does your awareness have at the moment? Alert? Scattered? Dull? What? Find your own word that seems to capture your current state of mind... Good.
- Now, before we start the body scan, take three deep breaths. Breathe in through your nose deeply but comfortably. Don't strain. Then breathe out through your mouth, and as you do so, let your body tilt back a fraction and allow yourself to make an audible sound – the kind of sigh you might make as you lie back in a lovely hot bath at the end of a hard day. Aaaaaaahhhh. Good; and again. And again. Good. Let your body gently and naturally relax a little. Don't force it. These are your three sighs.
- Now take your attention to your feet. Feel the pressure of the ground. See if you can feel what shape that pressure area makes on the soles of your feet. Notice any other sensations: temperature, tightness, tingling. Be aware of whatever's there. Good. Now let your attention flow up your lower legs to your knees. Notice any feelings in your calves... your shins... your knees. Fine. Now be aware of your thighs. See if you can feel the state of those big muscles. Notice any

sensations of pressure or temperature where the seat touches the backs of your legs, or where your hands are resting... OK, now let your attention go to your buttocks and your pelvis. Just be aware of whatever sensations you find there... Good.

- Now be aware of your lower back. Any aching or tension anywhere there? OK, now let your attention flow up your back into the muscles of your shoulders. See if you are holding your shoulders more stiffly than they need to be. Any sensations there? See how accurately you can localize the sensations. Let your shoulders drop a little if they want to... Good. Now be aware of your arms: the shoulder joints... upper arms... elbows... forearms... wrists... hands... fingers. Feel the sensations in your fingers... Fine. Now take your attention back up into your neck. Again notice any stiffness or tension... Let your attention move up the back of your head... over the top of your head... into your forehead... your temples. Be aware for a moment of any sensations behind your closed eyelids... be aware of your nose... cheeks... mouth... jaw... chin. See if there's any stiffness or tension in your face that wants to relax a little. Let your jaw soften... Great.

- Now take your attention into your torso, and be aware of your breathing for a few moments... Don't try to change or control it. Just watch your breathing as it is happening naturally, right now. Notice where you feel the sensations of expanding and contracting most strongly. Are you breathing from your stomach or your chest?... Is your breathing deep or shallow... fast or slow... regular or irregular... Good.

- Now just be aware of your whole body. Feel your awareness filling your body like the warm rays of the sun, relaxing and softening you... OK, now check out your general state again. Notice if you are feeling any calmer, or quieter, or more relaxed... Be honest. Report to yourself what you find... How does your body feel?... What is your mood now?... What is the quality of your mind like?...

- OK. If you are feeling a little more relaxed, use one corner of your mind to really notice what being relaxed feels like in your body... in your feelings... in your state of mind. Feel as if you are making a vivid mental note – as if you were deliberately stamping this impression on your memory – so you will recognize this state when it happens again... Good. Now see if you can let a word or a phrase bubble up that seems to catch something of this general quality. 'Peaceful'? 'Relaxed'? 'Quiet'? Let your own label come to you. Make a conscious link between this label and the memory of this state, so that in future you can use the label as your password to access this state whenever you want... Say to yourself: 'Aaahh... so this is what [your label] feels like.' Good.

- In a moment you can open your eyes and come back... Fine... See if you can bring that feeling back with you for a few minutes... OK, come back now.

People's reactions to exercises like this vary enormously, especially the first time. Some feel more peaceful than they have felt in years and find it hard to come back. A few go into a kind of trance for a while. A few, for a variety of different reasons, find it upsetting. (Just giving themselves permission to relax may allow feelings to come to the surface that they have been trying to suppress.) A few find it very difficult, even irritating. Especially if it didn't seem to work terribly well for you the first time, it is worthwhile persisting. The experience of the exercise can change dramatically from one time to another.

It is especially worth persisting with trying to establish the 'password'. At odd moments during the day, when you have a minute to yourself, try sitting down, closing your eyes, taking the three deep breaths (with the sigh), and saying your password to yourself. With a little practice you will find that this is sufficient to drop you back into the relaxed-alert state.

There are people who find it difficult to relax in this gentle, direct way, and they may need, at first, to find relaxation on the rebound from some more vigorous activity, or by deliberately increasing their physical tension before letting go. Try stretching out to make your body cover the largest area it can for a minute, then scrunching it up to occupy the smallest possible space for another minute, before allowing it to relax again. Or you may need to go for a good hard run. However you do it, being able to recognize and access that relaxed but still alert state of mind is one of the gateways to creativity.

The Creative Thinking Plan
Part One at a glance

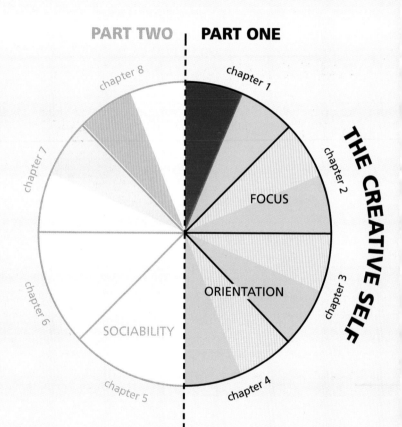

PART TWO | PART ONE

chapter 8

chapter 7

chapter 6

chapter 5

chapter 1

chapter 2

chapter 3

chapter 4

THE CREATIVE SELF

FOCUS

ORIENTATION

SOCIABILITY

KEY:

First way – Habits of mind

Second way – States of mind

Third way – Creative techniques

Fourth way – Creative contexts

PART ONE

The creative self

Change your habits
and you change
your mind

Chapter 1
Be creative: free your habits of mind

- Developing deep awareness
- The value of uncertainty
- Learning to ask questions
- The role of creative discomfort
- How to enjoy the creative process
- How to get out of your own way
- Changing your perspective
- The quest for self knowledge

'Show me a man or a woman who cannot stand mysteries and I will show you a fool, a clever fool perhaps, but a fool just the same.'

Raymond Chandler

Read any book about the dispositions required by a person to be successful and you will find words such as ambition, confidence and entrepreneurship. But to be creative you need to develop certain habits of mind that are not necessarily automatically associated with success. These are the first essential steps to take if you are seeking to revitalize your creativity.

By habits we mean your default mode of being, the kind of things you do when no one is looking and without stopping to think. The creative habits we are talking about include the ability to tolerate uncertainty, being open-minded, risk-taking, questioning, being patient, deferring judgement, being resilient and showing empathy. Habits like these underpin creativity.

Your mental temperament is much more flexible than was once thought. So allowing yourself to say 'I could not possibly change the way I go about things' is not an option if you want to be creative. In an increasingly uncertain world you need to come to terms with a curious fact: uncertainty requires you to be creative, and creativity requires uncertainty. Creativity and uncertainty are symbiotic, feeding off each other. Yet while most people would see 'creative' as a good thing, many have less positive associations with the idea of uncertainty. For some people uncertainty suggests powerlessness, lack of control, even weakness. We will show you that, in many situations, to be uncertain is the smart response.

Practising some of the habits we suggest in this chapter will, slowly but surely, help you to be more creative in all areas of your life. Of course, anything that involves developing your creativity inevitably involves personal growth and an element of risk. But as you work your way through this first chapter, try to choose issues and problems that do not take you too far out of your comfort zone. If you choose to explore things that are personal or emotional in the exercises, you might not manage to get through them and might end up feeling distressed. We suggest you choose problems that are neither so slight that they aren't of any real importance, nor so laden with anxiety that they cause you pain. Later on, once you have grown in confidence with the techniques, you might want to come back and try some of the exercises again using more personal or more difficult 'stuff'.

◼ Hanging out in the fog

It is an essential starting point in our thinking about creativity that we need to be able to tolerate uncertainty and expect complexity. We need to be able to say 'I don't know' with confidence and to enjoy hanging out in the fog, unable immediately to see where we are, where we are going or even who is with us on the journey.

People who are uncomfortable with uncertainty are more afraid to admit to being confused or stuck and so feel compelled to appear more certain, confident and decisive than they really are. They would rather leap to a conclusion, and focus their energies on defending it, than spend time feeling out the complexity of the situation and letting it resonate with the deeper stores of knowledge and experience they have inside.

They often ask poor questions because they are too intent on assuaging their anxiety by finding an (apparent) answer. Their 'decisiveness' is not so much a mark of quick-wittedness or strength of character as of their feelings of shame or inadequacy in the face of real difficulty.

Malcolm Westcott at Vassar College in America set people problems in which they could request as many additional clues as they wished before they volunteered an answer. He found that people fell into four groups, depending on how many clues they asked for, and whether their solutions tended to be correct or incorrect.

Those who were often right on the basis of only a little information he called the 'successful intuitives'. Those who needed much more information before they offered a correct solution he called the 'cautious successes'. The 'wild guessers' didn't ask for the additional information and were often wrong, while the 'cautious failures' had poor scores despite having requested many clues.

When Westcott gave these four groups various personality tests, he found marked differences. Most significantly, the successful intuitives 'explore uncertainties and entertain doubts far more than the other groups do, and they live with these doubts and uncertainties without fear'. In other words, they possess a habit of mind that the poet Keats called 'negative capability' – the ability to remain 'in uncertainties, mysteries, doubts, without any irritable reaching after fact and reason'.

Many things are uncertain and mysterious today just as they were for Keats. What about 'doubts'? There is debilitating doubt, which paralyzes you and undermines your resolve. And then there is quizzical doubt, which is allowing yourself to entertain the possibility that things might not be as you had thought them to be. Quizzical doubt is a really useful habit to acquire.

Or you may be 'irritable'. If an itch is irritating, you have got to scratch it. If next door's music is irritating you, you have to do something about it: bang on the wall, put in your earplugs, or get yourself righteously upset. It's difficult to be creative if you are feeling irritable.

And finally 'facts and reason'. These are our two impostors for creative intelligence. If you cannot bear to hang out in the fog, you reach for what you know to plug the gap. You try to be knowledgeable. You try to be clever.

NOW TRY THIS: Confess your ignorance

Take a moment to reflect on Westcott's experiment. Into which group do you think you might fall? Can you recall the last time you said 'I don't know'? When was the last time you said you didn't understand something, or know what to do, in a meeting at work? Can you vividly recall times when your attempts to look more knowledgeable were exposed? How did you feel?

Imagine you are talking to someone with a strong accent over a bad telephone line or in a noisy restaurant. How many times would you ask them to repeat something you didn't understand? Can you imagine feeling comfortable saying, 'I'm sorry, I still don't know what you are saying'? At what point do you give up and start to make agreeing noises, or nod and smile like an idiot, hoping you can get away with the impression of understanding? Does it make you angry or uncomfortable when you are in a conversation where people keep asking you if you have read a string of 'wonderful' books – and expressing increasing surprise when you dare to admit you haven't? Do you tend to express opinions more confidently than you really feel?

Do you find it easier to admit your uncertainty privately to yourself than to others? Or do you sometimes hide it even from yourself? Are you more willing to admit your ignorance or confusion in some situations than others? Who can you admit it to? Do you feel the need to look knowledgeable and confident to your spouse? Your children? Your work colleagues? Your manager? Your friends?

How challenging have you found these questions? Were you able to take them seriously? How honest were you? The greater your tendency to slide over them, or to denigrate the exercise itself, the more likely you are to benefit from doing it. Sorry!

Here is a task for you. Practise saying, 'I don't know.' To start with, don't choose situations where the consequences may really be serious. Find three opportunities to expose your uncertainty each day. Dither over your choice in a restaurant. Raise the subject of your next holiday with your partner, and try to stay publicly uncertain for as long as you can. See if you can initiate such a game with your children or grandchildren, and see if you can enjoy it.

Gradually build up your willingness to ask questions or reveal your ignorance in work situations. Start looking for opportunities to spend more time discussing the question, and not rushing into decisions and action plans. Notice how those around you respond to these changes in you.

◼ Enjoy being confused

'If you're not confused, you're not thinking clearly.'

Tom Peters

Interesting questions frequently arrive in an unclear state. Interesting problems are often too complex to take in quickly. The experience of entertaining an unclear question, or trying to get your brain round a complicated problem, or not knowing what to do because what you confidently thought was going to work didn't – that experience is called 'being confused'. When life is difficult, it is very smart to be confused. Being averse to confusion, and having to do something about it in order to feel better, is stupid. If you don't like being confused, you are compelled to be in a hurry to solve it and neaten it up – and in your haste you may miss the nub of it.

People find out more about complicated, novel situations when they can allow themselves to be confused. In one study, people were given an intricate computer environment to try to figure out. They just had to play with it and see what happened. The ways in which this virtual world behaved were sometimes counter-intuitive. Some of the participants in the study were given pre-training on a problem that looked similar, but actually had no rules at all: the computer's responses to the operator's instructions were completely random. The people who had had this experience learnt how to operate the 'test environment' faster than those who had not. The pre-training had effectively taught them to give up their preconceptions, so they were able to interact more open-mindedly, and thus discover the unusual patterns that were there more quickly. By inducing a 'don't-know mind', the experimenters effectively made their volunteers smarter.

NOW TRY THIS: Creating a 'don't know' mind

Here is a meditation that is very good at clearing the mind of what you know in order to allow space for what you don't know to come in. Its source is a Korean Zen master, Seung Sahn Sunim, now resident in the USA.

Sit quietly. Close your eyes. Make your 'three sighs' (see pages 16–19). Relax. Now breathe in and out more deeply than normal. Breathe in slowly till your lungs are comfortably full. Try to fill every part of your lungs from low down in your stomach right up to the top of your chest. Hold the breath for a moment, and then let it out in a slow steady stream until your lungs are fully deflated. Wait for a second or two before allowing the new breath to start flowing in. Breathe with a nice regular rhythm.

Now, on each in-breath, say to yourself, 'Clear mind,' repeating the phrase slowly two or three times so it fills up the time each in-breath takes. Then, on the out-breath, say to yourself, 'Don't know'. Draw out the 'don't' and the 'know' so they fill the time the out-breath takes. Feel as if your mind is discharging all its accumulated knowledge, opinions and expectations, so that, when you get to the end of the out-breath, your mind is alert and open, but still and empty. Allow yourself, for a moment, to feel as if you don't know anything. Feel like an alert idiot. Then start the in-breath again.

Do this for five minutes, or as long as you've got. It is an extremely valuable exercise to do just before you embark on a meeting or a conversation where you don't know what is going to happen. It gets you ready to think freshly, and to allow new possibilities to bubble up.

Admitting you don't know the answer can be risky at a time when our society is becoming increasingly risk-averse. Yet, not surprisingly, risk-taking is an essential part of the creative process. You might just have to go out on a limb for a while.

Salman Rushdie, who knows what it is to risk his life through art, says: 'The real risks for any artist are taken… in pushing the work to the limits of what is possible, in the attempt to increase the sum of what it is possible to think. Books become good when they go to this edge and risk falling over it – when they endanger the artist by reason of what he has, or has not, artistically dared.'

Few people would aspire to be in Rushdie's shoes. But that should not stop you from embracing risk a little more willingly. And if you are really worried, try this exercise as an antidote to taking the easy, familiar route.

NOW TRY THIS: Worst-case thinking

Sometimes we are just too fearful by half. Yet this may be precisely because we have not thought enough about how fearful we could become if the worst option really happened.

Try this. Close your eyes. Think of the most risky thing you are doing in your life at present. Now imagine what would happen if it went wrong. Picture the situation. You're not trying hard enough! Think some more. If you had summoned up a minor accident, turn it into a drama. Then into a crisis and then make it worse still.

How likely is it that any of these scenarios you have created will happen? Not very? Rather remote? Sometimes it helps to stare real disaster in the face: it may actually give you confidence to take risks.

How to ask good questions

'My mother made me a scientist without ever intending to. Every other Jewish mother in Brooklyn would ask her child after school: "So, did you learn anything today?" But not my mother. "Izzy," she would say, "did you ask a good question today?"'

Isidor Isaac Rabi

While society seems to value smart answers, creative people, such as the Nobel laureate above, know that it is the questions that matter more. Often we need to find the real problem, and not the solution that people think is required.

Good ideas come in response to good questions. A good idea offers a solution to a problem, or at least a fruitful way forward when you are blocked. But you have to care about the problem. You have to want to make progress. There has to be a question there somewhere, even if it is not very clearly formulated, which gives purpose to your enquiry, and against which the goodness of an idea can be judged. But not all questions are equally productive. Some are trivial and some are nonsensical. So what makes a good question? What kinds of questions demand the kind of deep-down smartness that we have been talking about?

Here is a list of questions. Ponder them and see if you can pick out the ones that seem to you to be 'good' questions. Are there different kinds of good questions? What do they have in common?

What time is it?

What do occasional tables do the rest of the time?

Who won World War II?

Should I take that job in Canberra?

Have you read any good books lately?

Can you teach managers to use their intuition more effectively?

What is 2 x 2?

What shall we have for dinner?

What is the meaning of life?

Why won't the car start?

Why do people read horror stories?

What is the speed of sound?

Who killed Cock Robin?

What shall we do when Thomas goes off to university?

Why do kamikaze pilots wear helmets?

Some questions are pretty straightforward. You ask me what the time is. I look at my watch and tell you. Of course, even here there is room to mess things up a bit. I might respond, if I am feeling difficult, by asking you, 'Where?' Two times two is four – unless you want to get fancy and start asking about different number systems. (You get a different answer in 'octal'.) And, provided you know the nursery rhyme, there is only one right answer to the puzzle of Cock Robin – 'I, said the sparrow, with my bow and arrow.'

Some questions are asked not in order to get a specific answer, but as a general probe. Asking someone at a party about their reading material is not usually a request for suggestions so much as a broad stimulus for conversation.

At the other end of the spectrum are questions that are, in principle, unanswerable, or based on false assumptions, or not meant to be answered.

The question about the occasional tables is a 'good' philosophical question if it makes you laugh, but you are not expected to go away and worry about it. Questions about the meaning of life might be either desperately important (to someone feeling badly depressed) or beside the point (in the middle of a drunken and hilarious party game). But such questions may also be 'bad' questions in the sense that they are too grand, too all-inclusive, to be capable of being given a proper answer.

Questions like 'Why do people read horror stories?' or 'Can you teach managers to use their intuition better?' are too meaty for most of us. They need some thinking about and unpacking, and how to go about answering them is not all that obvious. What exactly is a horror story? Do all kinds of people read them, or only some? If so, what kinds of people? Is it younger people, or men, or people with a certain kind of personality? Even 'Who won World War II?' can turn into a PhD thesis if you start asking sub-questions like 'What do you mean by "won"?' (Compare the post-war fortunes of the economies of Germany and Japan with those of England and Russia, for example.) Or: 'Who exactly do you mean by "who"?' The industrialists? The code-breakers? The military? And so on.

The questions about World War II and the horror stories are more challenging, and potentially richer, from the point of view of requiring closer analysis and maybe a degree of insight and ingenuity as well. But they remain, at least for many people, rather academic. They may engage the passions of the researcher and her peers, but in a different way from a deeper worry like: What shall we do when Thomas goes off to join his sisters at university?

There are questions that loom up at you when life goes wrong, and the normal systems of control and expectation break down. Things are cruising along nicely, and then you are made redundant. You are diagnosed with a serious illness. Your child gets into trouble. A trusted partner leaves. At first there may be no sense of what the question may be: just a strong feeling of loss, or panic, or self-doubt. But as the haze clears, you may begin to see that the disruption of certainty and routine might constitute an opportunity as well as a disaster.

Ejected uncomfortably from a rut of habit, a deeper question may begin to form. What do I really want? Have I been truly living my own life for the past twenty years, or someone else's? There is the chance, even the necessity, to do and to be someone radically different. But who shall I be? Do I dare to peer forward into the haze of the unknown, or shall I keep my eyes firmly glued on the rear-view mirror of justification and resentment? Some of the most challenging, and threatening, questions fall into the categories of the 'midlife crisis' or the 'identity crisis'.

And finally the most tantalizing of all: those issues that have not yet crystallized into an askable question, but which constitute a sense of dissatisfaction, a barely felt unease, the shadow of a doubt. Why am I experiencing this reluctance to get out of bed in the morning; a faint feeling of apprehension as I drive to work; a lethargy that creeps up on me even as I turn into my own driveway in the evening? Am I getting old and jaded? Can I remember the last time I really felt happy? Is there something I'm trying to avoid? Or: what was it about that book that left me gazing wistfully into the fire for half an hour? Why do I find my children so hard to talk to? Here the questions are about whether there even is a question – and what would the real question be, if there was one? Can I – should I – allow the dissatisfaction to grow and intensify, or is it better to soldier on as if there was no question?

So a good question is one that is not too trivial, not too grandiose and woolly, not too silly, not too easy to answer by collecting more 'facts', and does not contain hidden false assumptions that make it impossible to answer as it stands.

Creative people value questions. You can learn how to generate good questions and how to get a balance between being completely open and being wholly closed. You can move between 'why', 'what', 'who', when', 'how' and 'where'. You may need a 'what' approach to focus on more practical solutions, for example. 'What can I do to overcome the situation?' will be more helpful, sometimes, than 'Why am I in this bind again?' (Too many 'why' questions will have you spinning round in circles.)

While recognizing that complex problems will not yield up their inner secrets easily, you can learn to persist with approaches likely to lead to solutions rather than ones that simply allow you to display preconceived ideas. All the time you will be on the hunt for connections that shine some light on the issue that concerns you.

Dare to question the questions

'There are innumerable questions to which the inquisitive mind can in this state receive no answer: Why do you and I exist? Why was this world created? Since it was to be created, why was it not created sooner?'

Samuel Johnson

Vague questions may need a little encouragement to develop, before you set about trying to answer them. One way is to ask questions about the question, as we did with the question about why people watch horror films. Dare to pull it to pieces and make it more complicated. Treat it like a nest of ants: poke a stick into it and see what kinds of disorder you can stir up. Or treat it like a kaleidoscope: shake it up and see if the pieces fall into a new pattern.

CASE STUDY

In one famous study, a group of art students in Chicago were given a large collection of objects to choose from and asked to compose and paint a still-life. They were observed closely to see how they went about the task, and their tutors assessed their finished pictures to judge which were the most creative. The best pictures were painted by the students who spent longest playing with the objects, played with them in the most creative ways, selected the most unusual combinations of objects, and delayed making up their minds about what exactly their pictures were going to be. These students kept an open mind about how the picture was going to turn out even when they were quite a long way into their painting. In other words, they lived most fully with the question of what their painting was going to be. Twenty years later, it is these students who are now the most successful artists. The ones who made up their minds most quickly and stuck to their original plans, failed to develop their careers as painters, and are now working in different fields.

■ Making space for troublesome questions

'Life is trouble. Only death is not. To be alive is to undo your belt and look for trouble.'

Nikos Kazantzakis

Living creatively means being sensitive to seeds of dissatisfaction, and willing to nurture them with patient interest and attention. Though some problems and questions are intimidating in their urgency, enormity or obscurity, a life without questions to pursue is a life without the pleasure and aliveness of learning.

Here is an exercise that will help you to uncover some of your own 'seeds', those little unsatisfactory things that may be bubbling just below the surface of your life. It requires, first, the induction of the relaxed, receptive, inward-looking mood we introduced on page 14. This is, perhaps, what Kazantzakis means by 'undoing your belt'. Then, into that quiet, reflective pool, you throw a question: a question about questions. And you wait to see what issues, some clear, some vague, some familiar and some perhaps quite strange, slowly rise to the surface to take the bait. You are not, at this point, looking for answers. Nor are you actively trying to formulate the questions clearly or neaten them up. Both the neatening of the questions and the search for good ideas that may help to answer them can come later. You are simply making a space in which queries, quandaries, doubts and issues that are already there can make themselves known to you. And as they do so, your job is to recognize and acknowledge them. This exercise is about clarifying what there may be on the agenda, not about making decisions and formulating plans. Here are the instructions to guide you through the exercise. Again, it may well be more successful if you get someone else to talk you through the process.

NOW TRY THIS: How to develop deep awareness

First, go through your relaxation exercise, either the long version, or the short cut where you make the three deep sighs of contentment, lean back and say your password quietly to yourself. Turn your attention inwards, and make sure you are really feeling in contact with your body. Be aware of your body as a physical entity, taking up space, having volume and weight and substance. If you are having trouble 'being in your body', try wiggling or gently moving different bits to encourage your awareness to take note of them. Slowly scrunch and unscrunch your toes. Move your fingers very slightly. Allow your shoulders to sag a little. Let your mouth soften and your jaw drop. Very gently rotate your head, and see if you can let your head find its own point of best balance on your neck.

- Now bring your awareness specifically into the middle part of your body: the part that includes your torso, stomach, lungs, shoulders and throat. Notice the rise and fall of your breathing. See what other sensations and feelings there are – however slight. Take your time to see how you feel generally – whether there is an overall mood or feeling. Don't try to *think* about what is going on, and don't use fancy words to describe whatever you find. Simple, physical words like 'tight', 'heavy', 'light', 'constricted', 'easy' and so on are best.

- Now ask yourself a very broad question, like 'How is my life going at the moment?' or 'Is there anything in my life that is stopping me feeling good?' This is the hard part. Do not try to answer this question from your 'head' or your memory. If anything familiar comes quickly in response to the question, just notice it and park it – then bring your attention back to the central area of your body and what is happening there. That's the place where the 'questions' will begin to bubble up. And they may take a little time to form – anything up to 30 seconds or even a minute. So use that quiet, receptive, patient mood that we practised in the introduction, and observe, attentively and open-mindedly, what comes into your 'middle' in response to the question.

- Usually something will begin to form, first as a physical sense, then as a more conscious intimation of what the issue is that is stepping forward to be 'heard'. 'Oh, yeah; there's something to do with my relationship with my sister that doesn't feel right.' Or: 'Mmm... I don't feel too good about the way things are with Tim at work right now.' What bubbles up may be something quite specific, or it may be very deep or general. Your job is just to get a sense of what the whole thing is about.

- When an issue or a question comes, don't try to solve it or answer it. Just gently note its presence, and see if you can place it in front of you. Be interested in it, but not too inquisitive yet. Don't dive into it emotionally. And don't try to push it away or deny it. Let the question know that you are not going to engage with it right now, but you are not going to ignore it either. You'll come back to it another time.

- When you've acknowledged and 'parked' the first question, go back into the body and ask if there is anything else on your mind, anything that's coming between you and feeling completely settled. Slowly see what comes, recognize it and park it. Keep checking back into the middle area of the body until it feels like you have recognized all the questions that you might want to give some time to. Say to yourself: 'Apart from these things, I really feel fine about the way my life is' – and see how that feels in your body. If there is a slight tensing or a kind of 'Grrr!', there may be something that hasn't surfaced yet. Have another look.

- You can do this exercise at any time to get a sense of what there is on your plate or to see if there is anything niggling away in the background that you might be avoiding or neglecting. But on this first occasion, see if you can come up with questions of different kinds. By the end of this exercise, try to collect at least one question or concern of each of the following kinds:
  - a practical issue that is unresolved
  - an issue that concerns you at work; something perhaps that you are feeling blocked or stuck about, not quite knowing how to proceed
  - something that concerns you about yourself; a habit you would like to change or a 'good resolution' that keeps getting neglected
  - a question of concern to do with your relationships
  - a *big question* that may be at the back of your mind – something long-term or strategic you are thinking about, or even one of those deep and meaningful questions ('What's it all about?' kind of thing).
- When you have finished this exercise, come out of your reflective state, and write each of these issues or questions on one side of each of five identical cards (so that when you turn them over and shuffle them around, you don't know which question is on the reverse of which card). Retain these cards as you will need them in a later exercise.

■ Overcoming barriers to questioning

'Doubt is an uncomfortable condition, but certainty is a ridiculous one.'

Voltaire

There are a number of blocks or resistances that may inhibit you from looking for good questions.

The strangeness of the new

The first – already mentioned – is the strangeness of being patient and becoming aware of your body in the gentle, open way required. This takes practice. It is a knack, like riding a bicycle, or simultaneously patting your head and rubbing your stomach. Anyone can get the hang of it if they try.

Everything's fine

The second enemy of enquiry may be the reluctance to make life more complicated and the temptation to dismiss the question about questions with a rapid reflex: 'Everything's fine.' You might feel, and with justification, that life is complicated enough, and there is more than enough complexity and uncertainty already. But it is also sometimes a good idea to stop and take stock of the questions you do have, and make sure they are the right ones to be focusing your attention on. It's possible to spend a lot of time and energy pursuing one question, only to find that it wasn't the real question after all. 'How can I get better at telling jokes?' may in the end give way to 'How can I get people to like me better?', and this might eventually turn out to be masking the deeper question: 'Why do I feel that I have to work so hard to get people to like me?', or 'Where does my feeling of social insecurity come from?' A question about how to tackle the next risky business venture may have hiding behind it another question about the need to continually seek excitement, or the origins of the gambler's compulsion to keep 'risking his shirt'. It is smart to devote your energies to the best questions you can find. (Following the train of thought inspired by these examples may remind you that nobody has ever yet been heard to say on their deathbed: 'I wish I'd spent more time in the office.')

The addiction to certainty

There is something in our culture, enshrined perhaps in the way we educate young people, that makes us want to be 'knowers' rather than 'finder-outers'. People learn as they grow older that it is good to be knowledgeable, and they lose the curiosity they had as small children. They fall prey to the confusion between being smart and being certain. Of course it is good to be and to feel knowledgeable, competent and in control. But the addiction to certainty leads us to shy away from uncertainty. And it is only by engaging with things that we don't know, or can't confidently control, that we learn how to do so. Whoever had a good idea if they could not first admit that they were in need of one?

The attachment to knowing

The attachment to knowing makes people feel anxious or ashamed if they feel ignorant or inept. They come to feel that 'being stuck' or finding something difficult means they are stupid – and protect themselves from this bad feeling by withdrawing from learning, or covering up their perceived inadequacy. But in a complex and uncertain world it is this withdrawal that is stupid. And it is very smart indeed to be willing and able to say, 'I don't know.' Little children are too busy finding things out to worry about losing face. Yet, even by the age of four, many of them have started to sacrifice their curiosity in the misguided desire to look clever. Toddlers are full of good ideas about how the world works, many of which don't work out. But that does not mean that their ideas were 'stupid'. The smart child doesn't worry about the trail of failed experiments she is leaving behind her. She is far too busy coming up with a whole lot more. If someone asks her where the water goes when it boils, and she says, 'Water heaven' – well, is that such a stupid idea?

The same applies to the smart grown-up. Here is the difference between a good manager and a bad manager. Both of them can potentially come up with four good ideas for sorting out the tensions between the sales and the marketing people. Both of them can discover, when they try their ideas out, that only one of them actually works. (It has to work this way: the problem is usually more complicated than they thought, and there are always going to be factors they have not considered.) The difference is that the bad manager can spend the rest of the quarter shoring up his self-esteem by endlessly explaining why the other three ideas were really good ideas, and that it isn't his fault that they didn't work out. The good manager, like the toddler, has moved on. She is busy coming up with four *different* good ideas about how to fix the next-but-one problem (only one of which may work).

Rock the boat

The fourth enemy of inquiry is the worry that asking questions will not only reveal your ignorance but unsettle other people and cause resentment. It may be the case that, to be really creative, you need to rock the boat from time to time.

NOW TRY THIS: What's bugging you?

Here's an exercise in generating problems and questions. It aims to remind you of the kind of 'creative discontent' that you probably had as a teenager. Look around at the world – your home, your workplace – and generate as long a list as you can of practical things that bug you. Some of the things we came up with the last time we did this exercise were shirts with buttons that come off after only being worn a few times, price tags on goods that you can't get off (especially on things you might give as presents, like boxes of chocolates or fruit), pictures that keep going askew, doors that stick in wet weather, half-dead things the cat brings in, newsprint that comes off on your hands, how to record good ideas in the middle of the night, wobbly tables in restaurants, yucky stuff that collects in soap dishes, commission on property deals and windows that rattle in the night.

Make a list of your own bugs. Try to keep going for at least ten minutes. If you can't generate a minimum of twenty you are in serious need of some creativity training. Try to make your bugs specific, interesting and, where possible, funny. When you are done, look back through the list and see which of your bugs might spark ideas for inventions. You may well find yourself inventing things that already exist. Don't worry. You'll probably hit on a few things that haven't been solved, and which could provide you (or somebody else) with an interesting challenge to pursue. Take one that seems to you to have some potential (and for which you don't know any workable solutions) and worry away at it. Have some zany ideas. See how far you can get in opening up the problem.

■ Patience: daring to wait

'Birth is not one act, it is a process.'

Erich Fromm

If you cannot bear to feel confused and you hate questioning, you are bound to be in a hurry and feel under internal pressure to come up with a solution, regardless of what the real pressures and time constraints may be. You are rushed and stressed not because the world really will fall apart if you don't solve the problem today, but because you need to re-establish your feeling of being effective, professional and in control, as quickly as you can.

From Milton Rokeach's research, we know that many people's creativity is enhanced when they are asked to slow down. If they are prevented from delivering their answer to a problem for a while, they will come up with a better answer. They are capable of switching modes if they are reminded or invited to do so. But some people seem to find this hard. They are compelled to make up their mind fast and stick to it. If forced to take longer, they seem incapable of paying any more attention to the problem, but instead fill the time with more busy activity. They think about other things they have to do, make mental lists of things to buy for the party on Saturday and so on. They get irritated by the very suggestion that they might be able to improve on what they have already produced, and impatient with other people who want to take more time.

Milton Rokeach concluded that: 'Some individuals, because of past experiences with frustrating situations involving delay [in having their needs satisfied] become generally incapable of tolerating frustrating situations. To allay anxiety, such individuals learn to react relatively quickly to new problems... The inevitable consequence is behavioural rigidity.'

Being able to wait seems to be a very important ingredient of intelligence and creativity generally; it is an important trait for you to cultivate.

In *Emotional Intelligence*, Daniel Goleman cites a study in which four-year-old children were left alone in a room with a piece of candy on a table for about ten minutes. They were told that, if they did not eat the candy while they were unattended, they would be given two pieces later. Many years later, the children who took part in this study were followed up and given a variety of psychological tests. Those who had been able to resist temptation all those years before were doing better in almost all respects. They scored higher on intelligence tests, were emotionally more stable, had better educational records and more enduring relationships than those who hadn't resisted eating the first piece of candy. Whether it is true that 'instant gratification' has become a feature of our credit-card culture, there do seem to be practical benefits in practising the ability to wait.

Being patient gives a leisurely quality to the mind that encourages it to be softer and more playful. It takes away the feeling of strain and urgency and makes it welcoming and spacious. Gardner Murphy summed it up thus: 'Both the historical record of creative thought, and the laboratory report of its appearance today, indicate clearly that creative intelligence can spring from the mind that is not strained to its highest pitch, but is utterly at ease.'

■ Delay your judgement

'In the case of a creative mind, it seems to me, the intellect has withdrawn its watchers from the gates, and the ideas rush in pell-mell, and only then does it review and inspect the multitude… Hence your complaints of unfruitfulness, for you reject too soon and discriminate too severely.'

Friedrich Schiller

The need to find security in certainty also leads people to judge any ideas that do come to them quickly and definitely, and to adopt an overly critical attitude towards the products of their own thinking. They are unable to harvest their inklings and imaginings slowly and gently, and must rush to neaten them up and decide whether they are any good or not. The tendency towards 'premature evaluation' means they run the risk of forcing a genuinely new idea back into familiar but ineffective territory. In the chapters that follow, there will be a range of exercises for noticing and valuing the vague, symbolic beginnings of ideas.

If you are trying to find your creative self, then it will be helpful to practise delaying your own need for gratification from time to time.

■ How to tolerate boredom and emotional discomfort

'I confess that I am often gripped by panic, the kind of panic that is felt by an explorer travelling through virgin territory.'

Joán Miró

You are not likely to be very creative and have good ideas if you are not able to tolerate some of the emotional discomfort that may crop up along the way. A good idea or an innovative project may begin to emerge only on the far side of a period of boredom or unease. And if you do not recognize the value, even the necessity, of going through that state, of finding the rejuvenation that may emerge, you may find that work, whatever it is, comes to feel flat and routine.

CASE STUDY

Composer Brian Eno regularly finds himself 'working entirely from the momentum of deadlines and commitments, as though the ideas are not springing forth but being painfully squeezed out'. At such times, he has learnt, the only way to find fresh inspiration is to take a 'holiday', though 'that word scarcely conveys the crashing tedium involved, for

I usually choose somewhere uneventful, take nothing with me, and then rely on the horror of my own company to drive me rapidly to the edge of the abyss'. For the first two days or so, he feels aimless and depressed. He does not have a clue what to do next. He arrives at the point where he is convinced that there is absolutely no point in trying to remedy the situation by digging up ideas. He literally gives up, cedes control – 'and at that point of giving up I am suddenly alive again... This feeling of sheer mad joy at the world... is the fresh clear stream at the bottom of the abyss.' Eno calls this 'idiot glee', and comments that he can sometimes get there even more painfully by sitting and working alone 'until finally I stop caring and, in a condition of total somnambulism, fall over something new'. But it's better, he says, to do the 'holiday/abyss thing' first, and then work alone.

Many creative thinkers have to force themselves through the pain of that preliminary descent. Without it, the attachment to earnest endeavour, tight-focus thinking and sensing, and their old habits cannot be broken. Gradually getting used to this feeling, and learning not to run away from it by filling yourself up again with busy activity, is creative. And it does not just apply to major works of artistic or scientific merit.

All of us could benefit by increasing our resilience in the face of this sense of being aimless or lost. Group and family therapist Robin Skynner used to claim that he regularly experienced this feeling on first working with a new family. Ten minutes into the first session he would begin to feel he hadn't a clue what was going on or how to handle the situation. All his experience and expertise seemed not to apply and he felt adrift, without his usual sense of professional competence to hang on to. But gradually, he had learnt not to fight this feeling. He came to trust that something would come to him, and eventually, after another half an hour or so, fresh inklings and ideas would begin to bubble up.

You can see the same thing happening with children on a wet day at home. At first there is 'nothing to do' and the spectre of boredom only relieved by computer games lurks. Banish all prospect of the silver screen and children's natural creativity begins to emerge. The old cardboard box becomes a den. Unread books suddenly seem interesting. New projects are conceived.

Being bored, from time to time, is good for your creative self.

NOW TRY THIS: Discover the joy of boredom

Take a moment to remember what you did and how you felt during your own school holidays. Can you think of any times when you didn't know what to do, you were aimlessly messing about, and then something emerged that became a good project or a fascinating activity?

The next time you feel yourself getting bored, see if you can – even if just for a few minutes – not do something to fill the gap, but sit with the feeling and examine it. How does 'bored' feel in your body? Is it sluggish, or restless, or neither, or a combination of both? See if you can explore what is so 'bad' about it. What do you think would happen if you did not escape from it? Do you feel as if it would just go on for ever? Before you give in to them, notice what your impulses are. What are your preferred strategies for escaping from boredom? A good time to observe these habits and tendencies is next time you are trapped on a long-haul flight.

■ Enjoy the creative process

Hard problems take time to unpack and research, and if you do not allow yourself to get gripped by them, you probably won't give them the time they need. And the processes of finding and refining the question, and of collecting a detailed database to amplify and surround it, will be truncated and coarsened if you are too eager for the result, the prize, the reward or the kudos. Even in the state of reverie itself, gently turning the problem over in our minds, playing with its elements and possibilities, we have, for that period, to be fascinated by the taste of the question, rather than grasping for the answer.

There are many studies that show that creativity is reduced when people's attention is more on the result and its consequences than on the question itself. We know that putting people under pressure to deliver, even if that pressure is in the form of positive incentives and rewards for success, pushes them back into overdependence on familiar lines of thought. And we know as well that extrinsic rewards can undermine people's intrinsic interest in the problem. When children are paid for continuing to play with a puzzle which they were happily playing with anyway, their interest in the puzzle fizzles out as soon as the cash stops coming. It is as if their intrinsic motivation is punctured and subverted by the overlay of extrinsic reward.

Here again, though, the creative position is one of balance. Whether at home or at work, our ideas always have practical repercussions. Most artists are enraptured by the process of creation, but they also want to sell their work. Managers may be genuinely fascinated by a technical or a human resource problem, yet it is a rare person who does not also have half an eye on a promotion, or how success would look on their CV. A senior nurse educator finds her professional doctoral studies challenging and absorbing, but she is looking forward to being 'Dr' as well. How are we to hold both types of motivation without the one suppressing the other?

Recent work by Teresa Amabile at Harvard gives us a clue. Two groups of eight- to ten-year-old children were asked to make up a story for a friendly adult, and the inventiveness of their stories was evaluated and compared. The 'extrinsic motivation' group had been told that they would be allowed to take pictures with an instant camera if they agreed to tell a story. The other, 'intrinsic motivation' group were not offered any such inducement. As expected from previous research, the first group told much less creative stories than the second.

However, two parallel groups had been given some pre-training designed to immunize them against the negative effects of reward. They had been shown videotapes of two slightly older children, Tommy and Sarah, talking to an adult about their school work, and discussing with her the way they handled the balance of intrinsic and extrinsic factors. For example, after they have been talking for a while, the adult says: 'It sounds like both of you do the work in school because you like it, but what about getting good grades from your teacher or presents from your parents for doing well? Do you think about those things?' Tommy replies: 'Well, I like to get good grades, and when I bring home a good report card my parents always give me money. But that's not what's really important. I like to learn a lot. There are a lot of things that interest me, and I want to learn about them, so I work hard because I enjoy it.' Sarah says: 'Sometimes when I know my teacher is going to give me a grade on something I am doing, I think about that. But then I remember that it's more important that I like what I'm doing, that I really enjoy it, and then I don't think about grades so much.'

The youngsters in the pre-training groups had two 20-minute training sessions on consecutive days in which they watched the videos and discussed their reactions with their teacher, who also emphasized the value and pleasure of learning for its own sake, and modelled ways of thinking about extrinsic factors so as to 'get them in proportion'. When *their* stories were analyzed, the reward of using the camera had not undermined these children's creativity. In fact the results were reversed: reward actually increased the creativity of the 'immunized' group. It was as if they had been shown how to think differently about reward, so that instead of undermining their intrinsic enjoyment and creativity it actually boosted it. Instead of seeing the incentive as controlling – someone else's way of trying to get you to do something they want you to do – they now saw it just as a bonus.

This result is important, because it shows us that the effect the reward or the acclaim has on how smart people are depends not on the presence or absence of the reward itself, but, crucially, on how they interpret it. If people see it as an attempt to direct and control them, they are likely (whether they know it or not) to withdraw their best efforts, tighten up and lose their creative edge. The reward either makes them anxious and they try too hard, or they frustrate the controller by reducing the intelligence and commitment of their engagement – even though they originally wanted to give it their best shot for their own satisfaction. They cut off their nose to spite their face. On the other hand, if you see the reward as ancillary to what remains an essentially self-directed engagement with the problem, and hold it 'lightly', it can make you even smarter. The creative person coaches him or herself into this second mindset. The creative teacher or manager encourages their learners to do the same.

■ Develop the art of persisting

Perseverance is essential in life generally and all things creative specifically. Complex issues may not be solved in your lifetime, let alone by the end of the working day. Good ideas often take time to incubate. Two-time Nobel Prize winner Linus Pauling once said, 'In 1935, a student of mine asked me, "Dr Pauling, how does one go about having good ideas?" I said, "You have a lot of ideas and throw away the bad ones."' As you develop your own creativity, you need to persist so that you increase the likelihood of your own ideas coming good. As golfer Gary Player once remarked: 'The more I practise, the luckier I get.'

A lack of resilience is becoming endemic in many schools, universities and workplaces. People give up too early, or fly into a rage if they get stuck, destroying exactly the kind of quietly receptive mindset they need to develop. Resilience is central to the creative process. As Jean Piaget said, intelligence is what you do when you don't know what to do. The same is true of creativity. Try this exercise to build up your resource bank of good ideas for when you get stuck.

NOW TRY THIS: Getting unstuck

What could you do to help you to persevere more effectively when you get stuck? Think of some times when you have found yourself apparently stuck. Make a list of the things you have done in the past that have worked for you and pin it up somewhere you can use it regularly.

Controlling ego: How to get out of your own way

'Truth waits for eyes unclouded by longing.'

Tao Te Ching

While personal engagement in the creative process is important, paradoxically, too much investment of self tends to reduce creativity. There are a number of reasons for this.

If your reputation or your self-esteem is at stake, it is hard to stay relaxed and playful. You might go into a focused state of mind, but start paying more attention to the outcome than the problem itself.

Your ego likes to take credit for successes, and needs to be successful, so it may direct you to go for the easy solution even if it doesn't really work, or try to force circumstances to fit the plan when the plan isn't working.

If a journey has been delayed by roadworks, an ego-driven person then drives like a maniac, taking all kinds of risk, just to avoid the apparent failure of being late. General Custer became so invested in his reputation and his invincibility that he *had* to fight Custer's Last Stand, even though the battle was unnecessary, he was ill-prepared and it ultimately destroyed him. Ego likes to direct and control things, and this forces you to get in your own way. It puts you in the wrong frame of mind for creativity, and limits your access to the richer connections of your subconscious.

One of the most unfortunate consequences of ego investment is being led into seeing things from your own point of view, and this makes it harder to adopt other perspectives. Our sense of self is made up of a whole knot of goals, interests, habits, preferences, concepts, beliefs and opinions. It is an entangled set of things we need, things we long for, things we fear, things we are used to and things we think we are. The more active this ganglion of self-interest is, the more our ways of perceiving and thinking are pre-set to select and deliver what seems to be relevant – and to ignore what is not. And the harder it is to stand back and notice details, patterns or perspectives that do not fit with those preoccupations. Yet it is only by adopting such a disinterested stance that we may be able to see what we need to see, and think what we need to think, if an unusual problem is to be solved.

Case Study

Meet Micki Pistorius, a 37-year-old senior superintendent in the South African police. South Africa has an unenviable reputation as the top 'serial killer' country in the world. (It has more instances of serial killing than any other country bar the USA, which has six times the population.) Though she has been with the police only six years, Pistorius is known worldwide for her uncanny success at bringing these murderers to justice. Largely thanks to her, the South African police now have an impressive clear-up rate for these crimes. It takes them three to six months to catch a serial killer. In Europe, USA and Russia, the average is two to seven years.

How does she do it? Not through any supernatural power, but through a refined ability to empathize – to resonate – with the minds of the killers.

Says Pistorius: 'They [the killers] do get into my mind. I'm not a psychic. I'm a psychologist. But there is some kind of sixth sense involved.' Colleagues are amazed by her ability to 'read' a crime scene, even one that has been cleared of the victim's body and much of the evidence. 'You just pick up the vibe,' she says. 'I just open up to them and they get into my head and I just know. I know what makes them tick and I know what they do. And the moment I see them, I recognize them.'

Micki Pistorius is a classic example of the good detective. She gets her own personality out of the way so that it does not skew her perception. She drops into soft-focus modes of both seeing and thinking. She contemplates and she intuits. And she allows the free resonance between her subtle sensing of the problem situation and the accumulated knowledge and experience of her own memory.

The value of empathy

Being able to put yourself in someone else's shoes is an important ingredient of real-life problem-solving. Successful generals do not just out-fight their opponents; they out-think them. So do good managers, negotiators, fortune tellers and poker players. Their perception is fine-grain enough to be able to pick up the subtle clues of body language and tone of voice that enable them to imagine another person's feelings and intentions. They are able to detect discrepancies between people's words and their private thoughts. 'He told me he loved me, but I just had a feeling that there was something wrong.' Sensing what is going on with other people is an important part of being well informed.

Empathy also increases the chances that the problem-solving ideas you come up with are Win–Win ideas, rather than Win–Lose. Stuck with only your own point of view, it is difficult to see how such optimal solutions are possible. Egocentricity limits creativity, and makes problems look more combative and polarized than they need to. If I can see how it looks through your eyes, we might see that we have a joint problem, and can search together for a joint solution. That is exactly the premise that people who work in conflict resolution start from.

NOW TRY THIS: Walking in moccasins

Native American wisdom says: do not judge another person until you have walked a mile in their moccasins. To get a feel for what this might be like, find a willing friend, and spend ten minutes shadowing them as they go about their business (trying to ignore you as much as possible). Stay close to them and try to mimic their every movement, gesture, utterance as exactly as you can. Move your eyes as they do. Copy their breathing pattern. Walk in the same way. Copy all their mannerisms as precisely as you can. After the ten minutes, swap roles if you like.

How was that? Was it easy or difficult? How attentive were you able to be? (To do this exercise well, you have to be exquisitely aware of the other person, of course.) Did this awareness of their physical appearance and behaviour give you a feeling for what it would be like to be inside the person as well? As you attempted to mimic their breathing and their facial expression, you might have begun to feel some of the feelings that went along with them. If you did, check out with your partner whether you were intuiting their inner world correctly.

You can do a version of this exercise in your imagination. Sit down, relax, breathe deeply and close your eyes. Now call to mind a person with whom you have some difficulty; a conflict at work, an unresolved argument, something like that. Choose someone you do not know very well. Bring them vividly to mind. Look at them in your mind's eye clearly and objectively. Now change places with them. Imagine that you are inside their body, with all their history, all their habits, hopes, fears and experiences. Look out at the world through their eyes. How does it look?

Describe yourself, as that person. How would you, as them, describe your appearance, your character, your strengths and weaknesses? What things are on your mind? What are you afraid of? What are your plans and dreams? How do you, as the other person, feel towards you as you? They might be critical of you… what is their story of your disagreement? Don't get into an argument with them, especially about whether their perceptions are right or wrong. Just get as delicate a feel as you can for what they might be. See how fully you can 'be' the answers to these questions. Don't think them. Live them.

■ Strengthen your self-esteem

While too much ego can get in the way of your creative development, there is, of course, a fine line between confidence and egotism. We need to have enough self-esteem in order to be able to function effectively. It only takes a few negative comments for our esteem to be dented.

As businessman Charles Brower said: 'A new idea is delicate. It can be killed by a sneer or a yawn; it can be stabbed to death by a quip and worried to death by a frown on the right man's brow.' The quest for personal meaning and personal growth is at the heart of our search for creative ideas. Underpinning all the habits we have been describing in this chapter needs to be a relentless quest for self-knowledge if we are truly to realize our creative potential.

NOW TRY THIS: Growing personally

What are you currently doing for your own development?
How do you prefer to do it? Alone or in a group? Formally or informally?
What might you start doing now that you have been putting off for a while?

We opened the introduction to this book with a fictional character, the lamplighter, who found a world with constantly changing circumstances difficult to stomach. Yet we have shown how essential it is to be able to be flexible and adaptable simply to survive, let alone be creative. In this chapter we have stressed the importance of developing certain habits of mind. Imagine you are painting a wall. These habits are the primer you put on to ensure that the paint sticks to its surface. Without them, you can paint away to your heart's content, but it will probably flake off in a few months. The same is true of creativity. Acquiring such habits is an essential step if you are to revitalize your creative life and work.

In chapter 8, we will be looking at the kinds of habits of body you also need to acquire. But for the time being let's move on to explore the ways in which you see the world and find out how it can be helpful to cultivate a state of mind in which patient receptivity is at least as important as focused looking.

How to look *at*,
as well as to look *for*

Chapter 2
How to focus: learning new ways of seeing

○ Opening the mind's eye

○ Freedom from facts

○ How to see the big picture

○ The creative power of 'could be'

○ Learning to 'soft focus'

'Give us things that are alive and flexible, which won't last too long and become an obstruction and a weariness.'

D.H. Lawrence

Having the right kind of attitudes and habits is important, as you have seen. But habits in themselves do not make you creative. Creativity has to come from somewhere. You need a rich stream of information to fuel your ideas and to help you get the fullest possible picture of what you are engaged upon. And to be able to receive this, you need to be in the right state of mind.

Historically we have defined information in a far too limited way, and as a consequence have surrounded ourselves with facts and figures. But in this chapter we will explain how you can increase your receptivity to information depending on the state of mind you are in. We will show how being able to move flexibly between different modes of *focus* will help you, too.

Focus is the first of the three dimensions of your state of mind that we described on page 10. We will explore the others – *orientation* and *sociability* – in later chapters.

▨ Fact fest or information overload

To begin with, let's look at the stuff that ideas grow out of – the information that stimulates us in the first place. One sort of information is the kind you find in books, newspapers and computer files. It is what you get on the TV in news bulletins and documentaries. It is the hard facts, presented and absorbed as objectively as possible. The most precise kinds often contain numbers. The population of the world will be 6 billion in the year 2010. The mouse eats two and a half times its body weight of food a day. Last quarter's sales figures were 6.7 per cent down on the previous ones. This kind of hard information is what you can rely on, communicate and preferably count.

The skills of gathering hard data from books, databases, primary source material and so on are familiar, and most people reading this book will be relative experts. But there are three ways in which hard information may not help you that much.

Facts are not feelings and they have no opinions

First, hard data does not tell you what to do. Frequently we are offered masses of very detailed bits of data, but for information to be useful it needs to be formed into patterns, and those patterns need to be interpreted. You can programme a machine to look for patterns, and you can give it a database in terms of which it will offer suggestions as to what its patterns mean. But eventually you only get out what you put in. Computers will look for what you tell them to look for, and they will assign the kinds of significance you have told it are important. They may help you work through what some of the implications of your assumptions are, but they will not tell you if those assumptions are correct or appropriate.

More facts are not necessarily better facts

Second, while some facts are vital, it does not follow that the more of them there are, the better. At some point the counting has to stop and the exercise of judgement has to begin. In today's world, we are drowning in information. The skills of data collection have to be balanced with even smarter skills of selection and discernment. One of the essential survival skills these days is to decrease the length of time between opening an email and deleting it (and even better, judging which ones you can delete without even opening). The skills of sharpening a quill, changing a typewriter ribbon or doing mental arithmetic are rarely needed now. The ability to sift relevant from irrelevant information is at a premium.

Too many facts can prevent action

Third, the current fascination with programmable information leads people to assume that all problems can be solved if you have enough facts, a clever simulation and a fast chip. Yet when a writer is blocked or a pianist cannot quite get the feel she is looking for, it is not usually because they don't have enough facts. When a child is distressed or a couple feel estranged from each other, it is not for want of the kind of information you can put into a machine. When a shipment of food to a disaster area is held up by bureaucracy, or neighbouring states are on the verge of war, the problem is rarely caused by the people involved not knowing enough. A greater number of facts will not resolve many of the predicaments in which human beings find themselves.

NOW TRY THIS: Sorting out your life

What five things would you most like to sort out in your life right now? You might like to look back at the five cards you generated in the exercise on pages 35–7.

How many of them are due to a lack of factual information? Which of them would be solved if you had access to more such information?

Think of three problems or quandaries in your life that *would* be solved by having more data, and three that would not.

What is the difference between them?

Are there different kinds of information (for example, about your own feelings and desires) that would be more useful?

Our key point is that we tend to ignore the valuable sources of the sort of information that cannot be put into words or symbols. Problems often arise because of beliefs we do not know we have. And much information is contained in the ways we see and feel. When people are asked to try to describe an array of unfamiliar faces, they remember them less well than people who have simply looked at them without trying to describe them. Why? Because most of the information in a human face cannot be put into words. We recognize faces largely on the basis of complex patterns of features for which we have no names. We only have a limited vocabulary for describing noses and mouths and hairstyles. So when we try to put a face into words, we are forced to describe features that are different from the inarticulate ones we actually use to recognize it. We have to shrink and skew the description of the face in order to fit our vocabulary. And a limited vocabulary therefore tends to make our perceptions more crude and distorted than they need to be. It is not necessarily creative to think and talk too much about the world we see – that gets in the way of fully sensing it.

For we 'see' through all our senses. We have to find coherence in all the data that floods into our mind, at the same time as we grapple with a store of memories, habits and concepts, much of which exist below the surface of our mind. We draw on them in order to give meaning to the present. What is this situation like? What does it remind me of? What did I do last time, and how did it turn out? Perception and memory enrich each other. The more fully we sense the world, the richer the records we lay down in our memory. The richer the store, the better able we are to make sense of what is going on right now. And consequently, the bigger the picture we possess.

NOW TRY THIS: How words interfere with what we see

Look at these drawings for a minute. To help you remember them, we have put by the side of each little figure the name of a familiar object they somewhat resemble. Now turn over the page and go and make a cup of tea, then, without turning back to this page, try to reproduce the drawings on a sheet of paper. When you have done your drawings, turn back to this page and compare your drawings with those here. Turn to page 73 to see the prompt clues again if you need to.

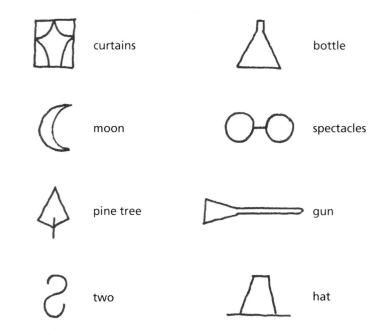

How did your pictures compare? You may well find that the 'helpful' labels have caused you to introduce distortions into your memory. For example, the figure labelled 'spectacles' tends to be reproduced with a little bow in the central line to make it look more like the bridge of a pair of glasses. If instead of 'spectacles' we had given you the label 'dumb-bells', you might have kept the line in the middle straight but thickened it.

And this leads to the final trap: that of assuming that we always have to build up patterns out of details that we have first detected and described. In a computer spreadsheet, you fill in the matrix with the facts, then look for patterns and meanings. But the human mind does not work like that. Often the sense of a pattern – a feeling or a hunch – emerges from our overall impressions, and only later are we able to break it down into its constituents. First comes the whole, and then the parts; not the other way round. Even when we as adults perceive a word, we do so holistically, and only subsequently, if we are obliged to, do we break it into letters. Take this example of a squiggle from which it is possible to make out a word even though the letters are not strictly accurate.

minimum

We are designed to see whole, meaningful patterns first, and details second. It is more important to know that you are in the presence of a tiger than a tiger's ears.

There are computer programmes now that work like this. They are called 'neural networks' and, as the name implies, they work much more like human brains than do conventional microprocessors. Some of them are surprisingly good at distilling whole patterns out of a range of complex experiences. For example, it is rumoured that a high street bank has successfully used a neural network to unearth the complex pattern of characteristics that go to make up the slippery concept of credit-worthiness. In this case, human analysts had not been able to come up with a model to predict whether someone was a good credit risk on the basis of their personal data. But when the programme was fed with thousands of real records of both good risks and defaulters, it was found to be able to predict future risks rather well. Yet – infuriatingly – the programme did not 'know' how it did it. There was no way of making explicit the implicit expertise it had developed. Just like the way real human beings operate much of the time. As philosopher Michael Polanyi summed it up: 'We know much more than we know we know.' And if we restrict ourselves to using only what we know we know, we are wilfully being less creative than we could be.

■ Soft sensing: the power of intuition

Being able to get an intuitive sense of the big picture without necessarily having all the facts and figures to back it up is a key asset in many practical areas of life. Often you just know when something is not right with your partner, or one of your children, or a work situation, even though you cannot put your finger on it – and even though, sometimes, the other people themselves do not know what is the matter. This is also true in a work context. A senior management consultant working for PriceWaterhouseCoopers told us that, in the early stage of getting to know a client, he is really just allowing his intuition to pick up clues, although he may well pretend that he is gathering hard data as this is what the client expects as value for money.

The ability to gain an overall sense of a situation, and to feel the way things are going before your competitors do, is a major factor in business success. If we could bottle the ability to have accurate hunches and sell it, we would be rich. Henry Mintzberg, the business guru from Montreal, says that successful managers are often those who can 'see the big picture', which relies on a 'relational, holistic use of information'. Economist Brian Arthur from the Santa Fe Institute says of Bill Gates that he 'is not really a master of technology but of pre-cognition: guessing the shape of the next game'.

A good illustration of the practical value of soft seeing comes from the hard-headed world of prospecting for minerals and metals. It is an expensive business, sinking a mine, and companies fight to hire the professional geologists who have the best track record. Yet the top geologists are unconventional and intuitive. Larry Turner at the Colorado School of Mines explains: 'The intuitive ability of good exploration-geologists basically manifests in their being exposed to very limited data, their continual mulling over of this data, and then arriving at complete and accurate perceptions of the whole – perceptions that are good enough to effectively guide the long, intricate sequence of operations required for discovery and delineation of an earth-hidden mineral deposit.' Ironically, however, executives of the big, senior companies so distrust the methods that deliver these invaluable results that they hire instead analytical, cautious, by-the-book geologists with whom they feel more comfortable, despite the fact that they rarely deliver the goods. They refuse to have the geological mystics on the payroll, but they then end up paying inflated fees to the small companies, which are the only ones wacky enough to give the successful mystics a job.

Our tendency to see information as coming in little bits of data leads us to look at the world in a tight-focus way when actually we need to switch to a broader, softer-focus way of seeing.

Everybody has the ability to widen his or her cone of attention and take in more information at once. But for some people it may take a little practice. Here are some exercises that can help you, first, to tell what your habitual way of attending is, and second, to practise soft-focus sensing.

NOW TRY THIS: Cultivating attentiveness

In this exercise, we want you to sit quietly and become aware of your own process of being aware. For example, see if you can find a place in which there are a variety of sounds around you. It doesn't much matter what the sounds are, though natural sounds – waves, wind, birdsong, animals – have an intrinsic charm for many people. But traffic and the creaking of the pipes when the central heating comes on will work perfectly well. It is best if there is no one sound that grabs your attention much more strongly than the others or is particularly annoying.

- Sit still, do your relaxation exercise and open your ears. Invite your mind to dwell in the world of sound for a few minutes. Just take note of what you can hear… Don't worry if your mind slides off into thoughts or other sensations from time to time. When you realize you have drifted off, see if your attention is willing to come back to the sounds again. Don't get into a battle with your attention – you may find that it has a strong will of its own. And don't start criticizing yourself, or the process, if your mind hops around a lot. Try to follow the instructions, and then take whatever you get…

- Now see if you can notice anything about how you have been attending to the sounds. First, notice whether you have been spontaneously naming or labelling them. Have you been compulsively pigeon-holing them? 'That sounds like a blackbird.' 'That's Tom downstairs coughing.' 'That's a funny engine… Ah! It's a diesel.

Probably a black cab.' Notice if there is a tendency to get frustrated or intrigued if a sound defies recognition for a while. Being able to hear voices, but not what they are saying, can be very tantalizing… Just notice the extent to which you have a general tendency to want to nail your experience down.

- Now go back to the sounds for a minute. Ask yourself if you can let them be without trying to categorize them. See if you can listen to each sound in its absolute uniqueness, without labelling it, or, if you must label it, beyond the point of recognition. Observe if your attention gets bored as soon as it has labelled a sound and immediately wants to move on to the next (or to some much more interesting and important thought or fantasy).

- Can you hear the sound as music, interesting for the instantaneous richness of the sound itself, and not for what it *means*, or how you *feel* about it, or what you want to do about it? Or do you need to have a reaction to the sounds? 'I like this one; I don't like that one; that one's boring; that one's beautiful…'

- Are you tempted to automatically discard or ignore some of the sounds and to latch on to others? Which ones do you discard? Listen again. Are there any sounds you haven't heard at all yet? What are they? Have you pre-consciously decided they are too trivial or too familiar to warrant your attention? If there are any sounds like this, see if you can bring them into the cone of your awareness. Give them your attention. Can you hear them freshly?

- Now notice if you are listening to the sounds one at a time, as a series of solos; or whether you hear them all at once, like a symphony.

- OK. To finish, review what you have discovered about the way you listen. Think about your everyday life: in the office; chatting over a meal; walking the dog… Do you tend to be in one mode, either detail or big picture, most of the time? If so, see if you can think of what opportunities there might be during the day to practise the other mode. Make a resolution to see if, from time to time, you can notice how you are hearing, and to experiment with dropping into the other mode: practise making your cone of attention broader or narrower.

Try this exercise at different times, when you are in different moods, with different types of sounds. See how variable your mode of attending is. Do you listen differently when you are in the car from when you are in the bath? At home compared with at work? Try to develop the habit of being interested in the way you perceive and the spontaneous way you distribute your attention. The more visible you can make your own perceptual habits to yourself, the more likely you are to see that you have greater flexibility than you thought, and to appreciate the value of attending in different ways. You'll naturally want to recover greater flexibility.

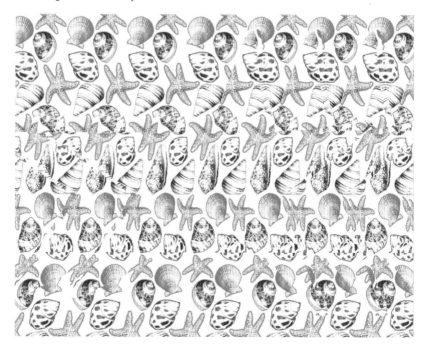

■ Seeing with soft eyes

The so-called magic-eye images, or stereograms, provide good practice at contemplating rather than scrutinizing – seeing with soft eyes.

If you look at this or other magic-eye pictures directly, trying earnestly to see the image that is hidden there, all you will see are speckles and squiggles. The more you try to find the pattern through scrutiny, the less likely you will be to find it.

To get the three-dimensional image to reveal itself, you have to 'not look'. You gaze through the details on the page, allowing your eyes to focus on nothing. This seems stupid: all you see, to start with, are blurry details. But if you are lucky, or patient, then the different parts of the pattern that are being received by your two eyes will fuse, by themselves, and then the 3-D image appears as if by magic.

Once the scene has stabilized, it then becomes possible to move into scrutiny mode, and focus in on different aspects and details.

Just like the use of the two light sources in the cave on page 14, you have to use the broad beam to get the overall impression *before* you attempt to home in on the constituent bits. Being creative involves looking *at* rather than always looking *for*.

NOW TRY THIS: Seeing with magic eyes

Spend some time playing with the magic-eye image. If you cannot get it to appear, bring the image right up to your face till your eyes are as close to the page as possible. They will not be able to focus, and will give up the attempt to do so.

Then move the page very slowly away from your face until it is a foot or a foot and a half away – and here's the trick – *without allowing your eyes to focus* back on the page. Hold the book still, gaze 'stupidly' through the page and wait patiently for a miracle.

If you get impatient and irritated, you will probably either give up ('Stupid thing! There's nothing there'), or lapse into tight focus mode again. Take a break, and gently try again later.

Becoming impatient may be one of your ways of making yourself less creative than you could be. You might take the opportunity to reflect whether this unwillingness to let things emerge in their own time is characteristic of the way you approach difficult situations.

When you've got the hidden image, congratulate yourself.

Here is another way of trying to strengthen your ability to look softly for patterns.

NOW TRY THIS: Big picture seeing

Here's a soft-focus exercise you can do any time. Just relax the focus of your eyes and take in the whole scene all at once. As you are walking along a crowded pavement, for example, or travelling on a bus, defocus your gaze and see all the movement around you at once. Be aware of what is going on in the periphery of your vision as well as what is happening at the centre. See the big screen.

Or look at a rain-spattered window. Track the movement of one raindrop as it makes its way down the pane. Watch it very carefully. Now shift focus and be aware of the whole window. See all the movement at once. Notice the different feel to your awareness when you are in this wide-focus, synoptic mode. (You could also lie on your back looking at the sky and do the same thing with the clouds. First watch one little bit; then be aware of the whole motion. Or do the same thing with the wave motion on a swimming pool, or on the sea.)

Bring both hands up so that they are about a foot out from each ear. Extend the index finger of your right hand and waggle it gently. Look straight ahead, and see if you can detect the movement of the finger. Move your right hand backwards and forwards till you have found the point where you are just able to sense the movement. Be aware of your attention being drawn to the periphery of your field of vision. Now do the same thing with the left hand. Waggle both fingers at once. Be aware of them both simultaneously. Notice whether you have been totally oblivious of what is in front of you, bang in the middle of your field of vision. See if you can include that in your simultaneous picture. Stop waggling the fingers. See where you have to put them to be aware of their presence when they are not moving. Is it different?

For an interesting variation, try doing the exercise in front of a mirror. Can you switch back and forth between the (clear) impression of the moving fingers in the mirror and the (hazy) sense in the corner of your eye? Can you include both? Is it easy or difficult? Do the clear fingers tend to drive out the more subtle ones at the edge?

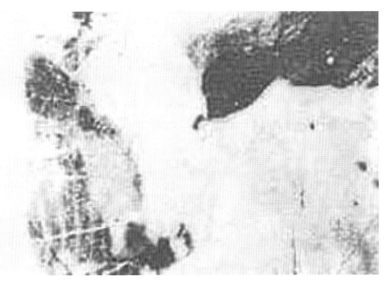

◼ Slow sensing

It is worth emphasizing the importance of patience. Experience does not give up its most intricate secrets quickly, and the acquired inability to let things emerge, to let situations speak for themselves to a brain that is not feeling pressurized or frustrated, is a very definite form of stupidity. People who are both clever and impatient are especially handicapped in any situation that does not conform to the usual rules, or cannot be accurately represented in familiar concepts. Learning attentive, open-minded patience is one of the most valuable ingredients of being more creative.

Sometimes it takes time for the pattern to emerge. Look at the figure above. What do you see? If you are unfamiliar with this image, you probably just see some meaningless splotches. Let yourself gaze at it without 'looking'. There is no visual trick to this, as there was with the magic-eye picture. It just takes time and the willingness to stay engaged with the image without knowing what it is, and without doing anything. You have to risk feeling helpless and stupid, because all your clever learning strategies don't work here. You cannot argue your way into seeing the image; you either see it or you don't. And if you do, it will be because your brain has found the pattern, not you. All you can do is feel grateful. Many difficult situations in business, in medicine, in teaching, in creative art and design, reveal their patterns only to the patient, synoptic eye – not to the busy analytical mind. Often it is very smart to keep contemplating a situation even after you think you 'know' what its main patterns and meanings are. You may have got it wrong. Your brain may have jumped to a conclusion, based on a cursory examination, that does not do justice to smaller details that may not leap out at you so quickly.

NOW TRY THIS: False impressions

Look at the picture below. Immediately you have an impression of what the artist has depicted. Now keep looking. As you collect more details, so the image may begin to change under your gaze. The young woman begins to give way to the cat, the stockings, the wine glass and the shelf with a plant on it. The first impression turns out to be less reliable than it had seemed.

NOW TRY THIS: Slow seeing at work

Take a moment to see if you can find analogies for the slow emergence of a pattern of understanding, and the dissolving of one pattern to be replaced by another, in your working life. Think of a time when you kept on looking at a situation and an interpretation came to you, either slowly or in a sudden insight. (It might have been a new project plan or a new structure or a new logo, for example.) Notice what role your figuring-out mind played in the generation of that new picture of the situation.

Now see if you can think of a situation in which things seemed clear, and then the appreciation of other kinds of information (maybe quite small ones) changed the whole picture. Again, was this an intellectual process, or was it more like a spontaneous perceptual reorganization of the way the world looked?

It can even pay to fix your attention as firmly as you can on something – a picture, a person's face, a familiar object – and really concentrate on it hard. When people are asked to fix their gaze on simple geometrical figures for long periods of time, after a while the images begin to undergo fundamental changes in the mind's eye. The brain seems to start to play with the shapes, breaking them up and reorganizing them in spontaneously creative ways. Likewise a word or a sound that is repeated over and over on a loop of tape begins to change into other words and sounds.

Many creative artists have found their inspiration this way. Rodin and Cézanne, for example, used this technique of 'staring' to encourage their eyes to see in new ways. Rodin observed: 'By looking at objects continuously you will be released from the typical way of seeing, and a less typical way of seeing develops.' Cézanne commented: 'Time and reflection change the sight little by little, till we come to understand.'

■ How to see beyond rational experience

How we act is not only, or even mainly, a matter of rational thought. We tend to see the world in terms of what is normal, or likely, or plausible (as well as what we need, and what we can do). Look at the shapes overleaf.

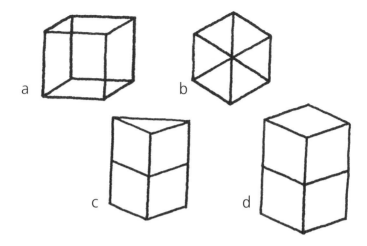

You are likely, at first glance, to see (a) in three dimensions, as a schematic hollow cube, and (b) as a flat hexagon with its opposite corners joined. But if you want to, you can see (b) as the same kind of cube as (a), viewed from a position where the opposite corners coincide. It requires a little effort to make the shift, but most people can do it quite easily. The reason your first impressions are as they are is simply a matter of familiarity. There are an infinite number of viewing positions from which an open cube would look something like (a), but only a very limited number from which it would look like (b). So the best guess your brain serves up to you is in the former case three-dimensional, and in the latter, flat. You will probably find it even harder to see (a) as flat. The plausibility of the 3-D interpretation keeps overriding the flat one. (Just as, for many people, the 'young woman' interpretation keeps reasserting itself over the 'cat-glass-shelf-plant' interpretation). On the other hand, you will also find that (a) keeps flipping, if you keep looking at it, between a cube that is being viewed from above and to the right, to one that is being viewed from below and to the left. Your brain does not have enough information to decide which of these interpretations to serve up, so it tends to cycle between both.

Similarly, look at (c) and (d). What do they depict? Without thinking, you are likely to see (c) as two wedges stacked up, and (d) as two cubes. But (c) could perfectly well be a wedge on top of a cube, and (d) could equally well be a cube on top of a wedge. You don't know. The information you have about the bottom whatever-it-is is the same in both figures. But just because it is more likely that the two whatever-they-are are the same, you unconsciously tend to see the bottom one in (c) as a wedge and in (d) as a cube. All other things being equal, the brain is likely to serve up to you interpretations that make sense in context. It looks for the overall pattern that is the most plausible, in terms of its accumulated experience, and may well massage the details to fit.

The brain is wired up to look for edges and contours, and it is well used to the idea that these very often continue despite being partially occluded by something else. We live in a world in which objects are regularly partly hidden behind other objects, and it makes good sense to see things in these terms. When you see the tip of a tiger's tail, it's better, on the whole, to assume that there is a whole tiger attached to it which you can't (yet) see. It's a good working assumption that the desk is still there underneath the computer.

■ How to break free of routine thought

The hard-wired expectations of the brain reach far down into the sensory systems, telling the eyes and ears how to go about their business. The optic nerves that carry all the visual signals from the eyes to the brain pass through a way-station called the 'lateral geniculate nucleus' (the LGN), where their information undergoes some reorganization. Neuroscientists have recently discovered that, of all the nerves that come together in the LGN, about 90 per cent of them are downward connections from higher levels of the brain, and only 10 per cent are carrying information upwards from the retina. We now know that these backwards connections, from the higher 'knowledge' levels of the brain to the lower 'perceptual' ones, are essential to the way the brain works and are found in all its component systems.

This so-called top-down influence on perception made good sense to our animal ancestors, and in many ways it still does to us. Under normal conditions it comes up with an interpretation of what's there that highlights the salient possibilities fast and efficiently. It short-circuits a lot of detailed bottom-up processing by making educated guesses about the situation, based on the brain's stored knowledge of what is likely to be there, and on what your current goals happen to be. At its most top-down, the brain functions like a busy doctor who asks you a few key questions to pinpoint the possibilities, and then does a quick examination to see which of the familiar ailments you have got. She uses her preconceptions to narrow the cone of attention down to include only those symptoms that seem to be relevant and exclude the rest. This diagnostic mode is fast and efficient – provided you are not suffering from anything unusual.

But if you have got something odd, the stressed doctor in diagnostic mode is likely to miss it. She will leap to conclusions, and may simply not notice the small detail, or the more subtle constellation of symptoms, which would have led her to a more unusual, but in this case more accurate, diagnosis. When the situation is not a routine one, too much reliance on top-down influences will over-narrow the cone of attention and lead you to reduce the range of your perception assumptions, in turn actually preventing you from solving the problem. Especially when the world is behaving in unprecedented ways, you need to allow yourself time to widen the cone and take in a greater amount of the information around you in a more neutral fashion. You need to suspend judgement, and function in a more agnostic, rather than diagnostic, fashion. Maybe the bottom block is a wedge rather than a cube on this occasion. It just might be meningitis rather than the flu.

The danger of first impressions

It is often smart to refuse to take your first impressions at face value. You need to have the ability to sit back, take another look, and see if there is a different way of seeing the situation – to go into 'could be' mode. When we say to ourselves 'That is a pair of pliers', we have adopted an attitude towards them that effectively prevents us from seeing them as anything else. If we had said, 'That could be (seen as) a pair of pliers', we are inviting ourselves to ask, 'Well, what else could they be?' Just a simple change of language invites us, in a whole range of situations, to store and use information in a much more flexible way. Talking to ourselves, and each other, in 'could be' language makes us much more creative.

Case Study

Scientists at Harvard have shown the practical power of looking at the world through 'could be' eyes. In one study, a high school physics class watched a video about physics after being told that it 'presents only one of several outlooks on physics, which may or may not be helpful to you. Please feel free to use any additional methods you want to assist you in solving the problems.' On tests of factual knowledge, these students performed no differently from students who had watched the video without the 'could be' introduction. But when they were faced with questions that asked them to use the information they had learned more creatively, the 'could be' students performed much better than the others.

In another study, students were taught a new type of ball game. Some of them were told 'This is how you hold the racquet.' Others were told 'This is one way of holding the racquet.' After a bit of practice, the weight of the ball was surreptitiously increased. The second group of students adapted their grip much more quickly and effectively.

NOW TRY THIS: Try out some 'could be' language

Call to mind a situation that is causing you difficulty, or where you feel stuck. It could be personal or professional. Write a description of the situation as you see it in a side of A4 paper or so.

Now go back and rewrite your description replacing all the 'this is the way it is' language with 'could be' language.

Be creative – don't just use the phrase 'could be' in rote fashion. Try to convey wherever possible a sense of creative uncertainty about how the situation might be construed. 'One way of looking at this situation is…' 'It might appear that… is going on.' 'It could have looked as if…'

Where there is an implicit (or explicit) 'always' or 'never', replace it with 'sometimes' or 'often'. And so on. Now reflect on the situation again, or describe it to someone else in these 'could be' terms. See if any new possibilities suggest themselves.

Tuning in to subtle sensing

'The impressions most useful for my purpose seem always those I was unaware of, and so made no note of, at the time they were taken.'

Robert Frost

Much of the information that is available to us is faint or fleeting or subtle, or it appears marginal to begin with. These small hints and cues can easily be missed by a mind that is coarsened by pressure, or too impatient to spend time gently exploring the situation, or which habitually overestimates the validity of its first impressions and rushes the process of perception in order to get on to more conceptual thinking. Yet the vital clue to a situation can often be contained in these trifles.

It is smart to be as sensitive as we can to the information that lies on the margins of awareness, or which may have slipped into our memory store un-noticed. The amazing feats of navigation of some of the Polynesian navigators, it has been claimed, were partly due to their having developed the ability to detect magnetic fields directly through their bodies (as migratory birds do).

Psychotherapist Robin Skynner has suggested that the phenomenon of 'love at first sight' may rely on the unconscious perception of small clues from the other person which indicate that he or she shares similar values or has been touched by similar life experiences to your own. We can articulate those clues only vaguely, or not at all, yet they culminate in a powerful feeling of attraction (or, in the reverse case, of aversion). And it has recently been demonstrated that the ability unconsciously to detect pheromones – apparently odourless chemicals produced by the human body – may also contribute to these powerful, but seemingly inexplicable, reactions.

Using your intelligent subconscious

You are responding to events that you do not consciously detect all the time. While driving, you have been totally immersed in a train of thought for several minutes – and then suddenly come to and take evasive action when a ball bounces out in front of you. (Where balls are, young children may well be about to follow…) But who was driving while you were miles away? You negotiated bends and traffic perfectly well. And who was able to detect the ball so quickly and re-engage your full attention? Your 'intelligent unconscious' was on duty all the time, picking up and making good use of vital, but routine, pieces of information that did not need to trouble your consciousness at all. Or: you are absorbed in a book and somebody says something to you. After a few seconds, the fact that you are being addressed percolates into awareness. 'Excuse me,' you say, requesting them to repeat the message. You look up, but they have gone. And then you get a sense that they might have asked you if you want a drink. 'Yes please,' you shout down the hallway. And sure enough, a beer soon arrives. In such situations you may not be sure if you got the message correctly – but you are right surprisingly often.

Being creative is about making as much use of all the information in which we are bathed as we possibly can – the non-verbal, the intuitive, the faint and the fleeting, as well as the clear-cut and articulate. Scoping a problem out involves allowing your mind to move gently over the data. You need to look *at* as well as look *for* pictures and patterns.

How you focus matters. It influences your state of mind.

Now let's explore the second of our three dimensions, the *orientation* of your mind's engagement. For the creative answers you seek may often lie inside you rather than being out there…

Prompt clues from page 57

curtains	pine tree
bottle	gun
moon	two
spectacles	hat

How to develop your creative intelligence

Chapter 3
Looking inwards: how to develop creative thinking

◯ Tune in to your intuition

◯ Discover creative visualization

◯ Why it's smart to be flexible

◯ Listen to your inner voice

◯ How to think straight

'How simple life would be, if it was as simple as we think.'

Michael Dibdin

So far we have been looking outwards, at the need to develop certain kinds of habits and at the first dimension of your state of mind: *focus*. Now we begin to turn inwards, to look at the different kinds of shapes and sizes in which creative ideas present themselves, and at our second dimension – the *orientation* of your mind.

Of course, many techniques exist for improving straight, logical, hard thinking. But they have been well described in many other books and we only intend to touch on them here briefly. As you will see, we think that, while useful, such hard-thinking skills also have their limitations. In this chapter we really want to explore some of the approaches that are more likely to ensure that you catch subtle and complex ideas. For, to be creative, you will need to heed other, more intuitive promptings from your unconscious. You will also need to clear out any unhelpful preconceptions you may have about intuition.

■ The role of hard thinking

Often, of course, hard, focused thinking is required for problem solving, and staying in soft, hazy mode will be counter productive. The message of this book is that you cannot boil creative intelligence down to one faculty. You need good information, but being well informed is not enough. You need to be able to see the forest for the trees – but sometimes you get trapped in one way of seeing the forest, and you have to go back to the trees again.

Because the role of deliberate thinking, based on clarity, articulation and logical reasoning, has been so overestimated in our culture, you need to be aware of its limitations, and to learn other strategies. But you need your hard thinking too; and when you do it, you need to do it well. Sometimes we fail to solve difficult problems because we think too much. At other times, we do not think enough, or we are thinking badly.

Clever people are adept at starting with a conclusion that they believe, or wish, to be true, and then constructing a fallacious but apparently plausible argument that leads to that conclusion. ('Many chief executives are male. All men are greedy. Therefore all CEOs are greedy.') People tend unconsciously to look for evidence that confirms what they already 'know' to be true. And people like to suspend their need for hard facts as it suits them. Many people, for example, take horoscopes seriously (between 70 and 78 per cent of us, according to one piece of research). They let selective perception and wishful thinking take over without even realizing it.

NOW TRY THIS: Explaining the data

Here is some information. Psychologists have recently demonstrated just how useful clear, systematic thinking is. Several thousand first-year university students were contacted around the time they were thinking about the courses they were going to choose for the following year. Half of them were asked to just make their choices intuitively. The other half were asked to be especially systematic and explicit in their thinking, so that they could clearly explain and justify their choices. They should draw up lists of pros and cons and weigh all the considerations carefully. When all the students were followed up a couple of months into their second year, the students who had thought carefully were significantly more likely to be satisfied with their course selections.

Why do you think that is so?
Take a couple of minutes to note down some of the possible reasons for the effectiveness of systematic thinking in this situation. Note whether you find the result surprising or unsurprising.

OK: here's the catch!
The results of this study were actually opposite to the ones we told you above. It was the 'intuitive' students who were happier with their choices. Now can you explain that?

How do you feel about this exercise?
Do you feel resentful or disconcerted? ('I don't know what to believe now. You've broken the implicit contract between reader and writer, which is to tell the truth as far as you know it.') Did you find it harder to accept the second 'fact', having done your best to 'explain' the first?

Ellen Langer comments on the research that underpins this exercise: 'We're all very good at working backward, and coming up with reasons to justify any opinion. In doing so we often box ourselves into a single view. I find that as students generate more and more reasons, they become more likely to believe that the 'fact' is true.'

How to 'think straight'

'Life is like music – it must be composed by ear, feeling and instinct, not by rule. Nevertheless, one had better know the rules, for they sometimes guide in doubtful cases, though not often.'

Samuel Butler

There is no reason on earth why people could not learn to think straighter. It is both incredible and scandalous that education does so little to improve the quality of people's everyday thinking. Many educators today neglect some fairly obvious points. Thinking straight can be coached; it has nothing to do with any kind of natural intelligence. But it can't simply be taught, like you can be taught to recite your times table, because thinking straight is not just a skill. It is a disposition, which can be acquired through practice.

When you are training yourself (or anyone else) to think better, there are a variety of general-purpose strategies you can apply, or questions you can ask, which may make your thinking clearer or more productive.

Here are some examples of different ways of approaching a problem.

- You could think of another problem that might be similar, and try to solve that one instead. So, for example, when faced with the task of planning a special holiday in a country you have never visited before, you could draw on project-planning skills you have acquired when faced with a new assignment at work.
- Or you might want to make a problem more concrete. To use the holiday example again, you could think about how you would organize and pack your suitcase to ensure that you took all the items you needed.
- You could turn a problem into a picture or a diagram and see if that suggests any new angles you may not have thought of. Let's say you are thinking of changing your job. You could draw a graph of the relationship between the key variables such as environment, money, journey time to work and so on. Or you could create a 'spider diagram'

of all the component elements of the problem and see if this helps you to find a way ahead.

better pension

smaller company

more money

less pressure

shorter hours

more responsibility

- Sometimes it helps to come at a problem from a different perspective. You could try to work backwards from the 'solution' (if you know it or can make a guess at it), as well as working forwards. Maybe you will be able to meet in the middle.
- If there are important facts you don't know, you could invent some to fill the gaps and see what happens. Computer simulations often allow you to vary the parameters in this way and see what the range of outcomes looks like under various conditions. But you can do it with pen and paper sometimes too. You might find that the missing information you have been hung up about matters less than you had thought.
- Often it helps to separate the problem into parts – chunking it down – and concentrate on trying to solve one bit rather than worrying about the whole thing.

These kinds of deliberate strategy definitely have their uses. But, at the same time, trying to boost thinking with such techniques can be counter-productive, putting you into an earnest, problem-solving mind-set (and pulling you away from the soft seeing and thinking that may be more helpful), and causing you to try to neaten the problem up too quickly. Hard thinking applied too soon or too strongly may have the same effect as pulling vigorously at the ends of a ball of string or a fishing net that has got tangled. You only make it worse, and harder to solve in the end. What is needed is a patient, attentive unpicking that seems, for a long time, to be making the problem more complicated rather than less.

Many real-life problems in management, professional quandaries, relationships and emotional worries are much more like tangled fishing nets than they are like mathematical equations.

■ Tuning in to intuition

'The healthy understanding, we should say, is not the logical, argumentative, but the intuitive; for the end of understanding is not to prove and find reasons, but to know and believe.'

Thomas Carlyle

It feels right. That sounds good. I have a hunch that it will work. My intuition tells me that I should give it a go. How often have you heard yourself thinking like this? Or are your inner voices more likely to be about logic, shopping lists, sums or hard facts?

We are now going to explore the phenomenon of intuition: what it is, what it isn't, and how, as a way of dealing with the world, we believe that it is both hugely undervalued and capable of being developed. For intuition is one of our soft senses, some would say our real sixth sense, without which we are not able fully to realize our creative selves. If we can work with it, we will be able to expand our sense of what counts as thinking.

But before we start, let's come at it in an intuitive way. Try this.

NOW TRY THIS: Checking your attitude to intuition

Close your eyes and relax. (Do the full version of your relaxation exercise on pages 16–19 or use the Three Sighs and Password short cut.) Now just bring the word 'intuition' into your awareness, and see if you can gently hold it there for a while. You might visualize the word written out, or you could repeat it slowly under your breath. When your mind wanders to something else, keep inviting it to come back to the word 'intuition'. Without deliberately thinking about it, see what ideas, images or associations bubble up in response to this stimulus. Stay in this soft-focus mode for about five minutes. Do your associations tell you anything about how you use or relate to the idea of intuition? Take another minute to mull over what came up.

You could also try the 'free association' method. Let your mind go soft, and sit with a piece of paper in front of you. Write the word 'intuition' in the middle and draw a box round it. See what association comes first. Draw a line at 12 o'clock up from the box and write the associated word at the end of the line. Now come back to 'intuition' again, and see what else comes to mind. Write that down at 1 o'clock. Come back to 'intuition' again, and so on.

Finally, use the same mood to mull over more directly the way you relate to intuition in your daily life. Ask yourself: how do I use the word in conversation? Do I tend to use it as a positive, negative or neutral word? Are there any kinds of experiences that I think of as intuitive? Do I tend to notice them? How do I tend to evaluate them? Do I ever follow my intuition? How often?

Call to mind a recent situation where you did or didn't heed your intuition.

- Get a feel for the setting.
- How did the situation turn out?
- Was following/not following your intuition a good/bad idea?
- Do you tend to be more trusting of your intuition in some settings than others: for example, more at home than at work; more with women than with men?
- Are there times when you know that you are acting or deciding intuitively, but feel you have to cook up a more logical-sounding rationale for public consumption?
- How do you tend to feel or experience your intuition?
- Are there kinds of intuition that you find easier to listen to, use or trust than others?

Ask yourself: how important, overall, has intuition been to me in my life? What is my general attitude towards it? Am I open to exploring it further, and learning more about it?

■ What intuition is not

Intuition is a much maligned word. This is partly because it has become associated, for some, with supernatural or divine knowledge. It may well be that people in certain 'states of grace', or who have been meditating for years, are able, in a sense, to see into the heart of things, in a way that is less clouded than usual by conditionings and desires. But, for the purposes of this book, we would prefer to avoid this territory. It too easily slides over into a mystical world of the supernatural where stories of predicting winning horses or explaining UFOs prevail.

Neither is intuition the same thing as instinct, although there may at times be a blurring of these capacities. We instinctively know that certain expressions signal either friendship or antagonism; that some gestures are threatening while others are not. We acquire our grammar without necessarily needing a rule book. Nearly fifty years ago, Michael Polanyi introduced the idea of 'tacit knowledge'. He describes this as 'that which we know but cannot tell'. It is the know-how (not the intuition) which enables you to use a knife and fork, ride a bicycle or know when the right moment is to approach your partner to ask them a difficult question (and how to go about doing it in a way that is most likely to lead to the outcome you want).

Without this special kind of knowledge, human beings would have to expend ridiculous amounts of their time and energy attending to important but basic tasks.

■ What intuition is

Just as in the last chapter you discovered that information is much more than facts and figures, so thinking is much more than using logic and reason. The best kind of creative thinking occurs when you are in a receptive frame of mind.

What did you think intuition was when you did the exercise on page 80?

When we talk about intuition we are trying to help you focus on what you can do here and now to handle your life more creatively. Put very simply, intuition, in our book, is the faculty that the smart mind uses when it is stumped and it needs a fresh idea. It is a perfectly rational and valuable section of the mental orchestra, for which there is solid experimental evidence.

In that sense, you could say that this whole book is about intuition: the central role it plays in an expanded, socially relevant conception of creative intelligence, and the ways to make better use of it. It's not sloppy and it's not supernatural: it's simply smart. Intuitions (the products of 'intuition') are neither always right nor always wrong. They are interesting ideas that may give you a fresh lead on a difficult question, and which need to be treated with a healthy mixture of respect and scepticism: 'respect', to let them come, and 'scepticism', to see if they really work as well as they seem to.

At a simple level, the classic problems opposite illustrate the way in which the world does not always respond easily to hard logic.

NOW TRY THIS: Finding new ways of thinking

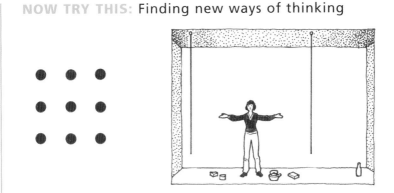

The 9 dots: Can you connect all the dots together with four straight lines, without lifting your pen from the paper? (See the solution on page 95.)

The 2 ropes: You are in a room with two ropes hanging from the ceiling. They are too far apart to be grasped at the same time. There are various small items on the floor: a can, a small carton, a kettle, a book and a bottle. How can you tie the ropes together? (See the solution on page 95.)

Of course, our lives are not made up of the kind of questions you get in puzzle books. Nevertheless we often have to take decisions or grapple with issues that bear striking resemblances to these kinds of problem.

Indeed, our ability to be intuitively smart has been central to our evolutionary growth. As part of the development of our species, it has been essential for humankind to develop a whole range of responses that are automatic and unconscious.

■ Creative visualization to get in the mood

If you really want to access your intuition, then your mood matters. Mood is very important, as you have already discovered. You need to be calm, open-minded and relaxed, and not stressed, judgmental or in too much of a hurry. Try this way of getting ready. It uses a technique called creative visualization that aims to induce the kind of mood that is sympathetic to the softer sensing that intuition requires.

NOW TRY THIS: Building your dream house

In this exercise, we are first going to ask you to relax, using the procedure on page 16 with which you should be quite familiar by now. Then we are going to talk you through constructing, in your mind's eye, a 'dream house', which overlooks a deep, calm lake. In this house you feel safe, relaxed, full of energy, and creative. It will be, once you have constructed it, a refuge you can always go to, to find your ability to be really smart (when you need to be, or just for fun). The house represents the state or mood you need to switch on your creative self. The lake represents your 'intelligent unconscious': all the resources you possess, whether you are aware of them or not, that you can draw on when you want to be at your smartest: the vast underwater database of the 'inner-net' (see Chapter 4), together with all the abilities and attitudes you will need. Once you are in your dream house, we will ask you to think of something that you would like to be better at, a sport or dancing, for example. You might like to spend a few moments thinking about this before you start the exercise.

As usual, this will work much better if you first make a tape, with suitable long pauses to allow time for images to form; or get a friend to talk you through it. Like many of these exercises, this one works well in a group, with one of you reading the instructions and the others following. If you do the exercises as a group, then you can share experiences and ideas at the end.

- OK. First, relax and turn inward. Remember you are aiming to find that state of mind where you are quiet and relaxed, but receptive and attentive. As you hear the instructions, let your mind come up with whatever it does. Take your three deep breaths in through your nose, and, breathing out through your mouth, make the audible sigh on each out-breath. Lean back a fraction (but still stay sitting more or less upright). Allow your body and mind to soften. Just for this time, feel that there is nothing special to do or achieve. Feel peaceful and at ease.

- Good. Now allow an image to form in your mind: an image of a house overlooking a lake. It may be somewhere you know, or somewhere that your imagination comes up with. Either is fine. Just so long as you feel happy being there, and good about the situation. Take a moment to look out over the lake. See how big it is. Notice what the weather is like right now. Can you see the far side of the lake? What is over there? Is the lake open or ringed with trees or other plants? What does the surface of the lake look like? What colour is the water? Make it a scene where you feel peaceful and at home.

● Now turn your attention to the house. This is your creative 'centre'. Walk around it from the outside and see what it looks like. You can even get the feeling of building it in your mind's eye as you go. Or you might find it all ready-made. What sort of construction is it? What is it made of? How big is it? You can make it as traditional or as unusual as you like. It's your private place. Where are the windows? Maybe there's a balcony or a big picture window. Where are the doors? Which is the main entrance? Create the front door. Notice how it is fastened or locked, and give yourself the key if you need one. Make sure you will have a good view of the lake somehow when you get inside.

● Now walk through the front door, and see what the inside looks like. There may be many rooms, or just a few; possibly only one. Focus on the room that overlooks the lake. Look around. How are the walls finished? The ceiling? The floor? Where are the lights? What are they like? What are the main colours in the room? What is the 'feel' of the room: light and airy; cosy and snug; what?

● Have on one wall – not the one where the lake window is – a kind of cupboard or cabinet. Inside this cabinet are your dreams, your aspirations. When you reach in, you will be able to find something – an object or some clothes – that symbolizes your ability to achieve what you would like to. We'll come back to that later.

● Now go over to the windows overlooking the lake. Look at the view. How does the lake look from here? Can you open the windows? Can you walk out? Get the feeling that the lake is easily accessible from this room. When you look out at the lake it is almost as if room and lake are joined. They are part of the same space. Feel that the house and the lake together form a unit that is both safe and mysterious. The lake may be full of things that are submerged, its contents and moods may surprise you, they can even startle you sometimes, but there is nothing in there that can really hurt you. The house is like the conscious part of your mind: familiar and under control. The lake is the huge reservoir of knowledge and resources that you don't even know you have.

- OK, now let's play with the cabinet of dreams. Open it up. See what's inside it. Think of a sport or a physical activity you would like to be better at. Find something inside the cabinet that symbolizes that activity. Take it out and hold it. If it is a suit of clothes, put it on. Imagine yourself doing that activity well. Look at yourself from the outside. See how skilful and graceful you are. Now be in your body doing the activity. Feel what it is like to move this way. Play with your newfound ability for a little while. Dance beautifully. Play tennis brilliantly. Whatever... Then take your new clothes off and leave them behind.

- Now let's explore the lake a little. Look out over the lake. Imagine that below the surface it is teeming with all kinds of interesting creatures. You can't see them till they jump out of the water, but you can feel the life, the unknown possibilities, that are down there. Now I'm going to give you a word to toss into the middle of the lake, and you will wait quietly to see what kinds of other life-forms it attracts. They might be other words, or images, or memories, or bodily feelings. Let them come to the surface in their own time. OK, the word is 'snow'. Drop the word 'snow' into the lake and see what comes up... say 'snow' quietly to yourself, drop it into the lake again and see what else rises to the surface... and again, what else wants to come up for your attention?

- Fine. That's it for now. Take a last look around your dream house for the moment. Know that you will be able to come back any time you like. It is your refuge, for as long as you want it. Go out of the front door. Fasten it behind you. Take a last look at the lake. Now begin to turn your attention back from the land of fantasy to the situation you are presently in. Before you open your eyes, remember where you are sitting and what you will see when you open your eyes. When you feel ready, come back to the present and slowly open your eyes.

How did you find this? Did it work for you? Some people are habitual visualizers. Many can sometimes be enthralled by it, and at other times left cold. A few people always have difficulty creating imagery to order, and find it hard to see what the point could be. But these things are not fixed. Being a good visualizer is not something you are born with. You can get better at it, the more you practise.

The voices of intuition

'I have had my solutions for a long time, but I do not yet know how I am to arrive at them.'

Carl F. Gauss

The answers to questions and problems come to us in a variety of ways. Some of them come as conclusions: the outcomes of well-ordered sequences of focused thought. But rational thought is just one of the languages in which the intelligent body–brain memory system speaks to consciousness. It works with such clarity and certainty only for a rather specialized type of problem – the sort that can be clearly specified and articulated. For many situations the voices you will want to heed are softer – the inspirations, insights, guesses, hunches and inklings which go to make up intuition.

Someone who is trying to decide whether to have another child, or what picture to paint next, or what to have for dinner, or how to find the confidence to meet people again after a shattering divorce, may find that hard logic does not help. For such problems, you need to be creative in different ways, and open to the different forms in which possible ways forward make themselves known to you. These other voices convey better the coming-into-being of ideas that are more genuinely and profoundly novel, and which may work well in situations that are messier and more complex. They do not (yet) arrive with a ready-made tale of justification, but their rationale, or their practical wisdom, may emerge over time.

You may, for example, have a blinding *insight* or a flash of *inspiration*, but not know where or how you came by it. You may make a complete *guess*, and be astonished by how right it turns out to be. You may have a *hunch* about which way to go that you cannot justify at all. You may develop a faint *inkling* of an understanding which stays vague and insubstantial for a while. There are other voices too, which we must be able to make use of, which we shall meet in the following chapters. But let us start with those we have just named.

To use these voices as smartly as you can, you need to be ready, willing and able to do four things. First you have to hear them. You have to know where to look, and be sensitive to the distinctive languages they speak. Then you have to heed them. You have not just to hear them but to listen to them; to be willing to give them time and attention. Next you have to respect them. You have to approach them knowing that what they have to say may well be worth listening to, even though they may not make immediate sense. And finally you have to explore them. You have to find out whether they are truly as valid or as useful or as robust as they might appear. You have to question them – but gently, to begin with. As we have seen, a harsh and premature interrogation under the bright lights of the critical intellect may shut them up, send them running for cover or strangle them before they have had a chance to develop and demonstrate what wisdom they might contain.

So, four things: you want to hear, to heed, to respect and to explore.

People vary in how attuned their ears already are to the voices. Some of them may be very familiar to you; others less so. But whatever your existing level of sensitivity, you can probably improve it, to your advantage. Learning to listen to the promptings of intuition just takes a little practice. Much of our learning, from childhood on, is concerned with developing our instinctive sensitivity to the world within and around us. We learn to tell our mother's mood from her tone of voice. We learn when we need to pee. We learn to tell when milk is on the turn, or when we are going down with a cold. Becoming more sensitive to the inner symptoms of our questions and quandaries is as matter-of-fact as that. It is no more mystical than learning to tell a chardonnay from a sauvignon, Brahms from Mendelssohn, or the sounds of a healthy heart from an abnormal murmur through a stethoscope. Doctors learn to hear those murmurs and tell what they mean. And all of us can learn to catch and interpret the murmurs of our unconscious – our intuitions.

■ Inspirations and insights

The most vivid and dramatic kinds of intuitions are those that erupt suddenly as blazing solutions or conclusions, carrying with them a strong feeling of 'rightness', but lacking, as yet, a convincing story as to *why* they are right, or *how* they work. One example is the work of Andrew Wiles, the Cambridge don who finally solved the mathematical conundrum known as Fermat's Last Theorem. In the 1800s Fermat, known as 'the Prince of Amateurs', claimed in one of his notebooks to have proved that $x^n + y^n = z^n$ has no solutions where n is a whole number greater than 2. Infuriatingly, he also claimed that he did not have time or space to write the proof down. Wiles, described by the newspapers as the proverbial 'shy Englishman', worked away at the problem in great secrecy and isolation for eight years – and then, in his own words: 'I was sitting at my desk one Monday morning… Suddenly, totally unexpectedly, I had this incredible revelation. It was so indescribably beautiful, it was so simple and so elegant… Nothing I ever do again will mean so much.'

The same can be true in science. Nobel science laureates have no doubt about the value of intuition and inspiration. From 1970 to 1986, when they went to Stockholm to collect their prize, every science laureate was invited to take part in a panel discussion on Swedish television during which they were regularly invited to share their views on intuition. Of the 83 scientists who discussed the question, every one referred to intuitive experiences that they said were an essential part of their research journey. (Six objected to the word 'intuition', but they too relied on exactly the same kinds of experiences that the others were happy to call intuitive.) Rita Levi-Montalcini, laureate in medicine in 1986, for example, said: 'Intuition is something subconscious, which, all of a sudden, comes out of a clear sky to you and is absolutely a necessity, more than logic…'

Inspirations and insights are the shock troops of intuition. It is no problem hearing them, heeding them or respecting them – they noisily proclaim their own validity. The problem occurs if you forget to question them carefully. Sometimes the feeling of rightness is very strong, and yet, on more detailed inspection, the brilliant idea contains hidden flaws. (Andrew Wiles published his 'brilliant' solution to Fermat's Last Theorem, only to find that it was subtly flawed. It took a further period of hard work before he found a way to overcome the problem.)

NOW TRY THIS: Is intuition always right?

Take a moment to reflect on this feeling of 'rightness'. Do you have 'brainwaves' and inspirations – brilliant ideas that come out of the blue? How often? Can you call to mind one you had recently? How did you respond to it? Was it self-evidently 'brilliant', or did it need checking out?

Can you remember a time when you discovered that a brainwave wasn't so brainy after all? How did you feel about that? Do you have a tendency to rush around telling everyone your great idea *before* you have thought it through? Does this uncritical enthusiasm ever get you into trouble?

Have a think about this problem. There are 23 people in a room. What is the probability of two people having the same birthday?

The birthday problem is a good example of something that is, in fact, counter-intuitive. Many people think the probability must be about 1 in 12 when in fact the correct answer is nearer to 50 per cent, or 1 in 2. We need to remember that our intuition can be notoriously wrong when it comes to probability.

■ Guesses

There are times when we don't know what to do. For example, you may be facing a decision about whether to move house or take a new job. You have talked the issue to death, drawn up lists of pros and cons, and you still don't know what to do. One common strategy is to act as if you are going to choose one option at random. 'If the issue is so finely balanced, I may as well just flip a coin.' OK: heads we take the job and move to Dubai; tails we stay here in Reading. You toss the coin and it comes down tails. You have 'decided' to stay. And immediately you feel a wave of disappointment. You realize that you really wanted it to come down heads. You didn't know it before, but this random event, this 'guess' about what you are going to do, brings up information from your unconscious that wasn't available to your more focused deliberations.

There is often more validity to 'complete guesses' than we think. In 1884 the practically minded philosopher Charles Pierce carried out a long series of tests, together with his student Joseph Jastrow, in which they judged over and over again which of two nearly identical weights was in fact the heavier. Of the thousands of trials on which they rated their answer as a complete guess, they were correct about 65 per cent of the time – more often than chance. Pierce concluded that we are subliminally sensitive to 'sensations that are so faint that we are not fully aware of having them, and can give no account of how we reach our conclusions'. Seeing the value of this, he argues that the ability to trust our guesses 'ought to be assiduously cultivated by everyman'. More recently, Pierce's conclusions have been replicated in various similar experiments.

Guesses are not always right, of course. But sometimes they can be amazingly so. Frances Vaughan records the case of a high school student who knew much more maths than she knew she knew. She was not enjoying her algebra class, and did not think that she was following very well. Yet when the class was given a city-wide multiple-choice test, she scored top in the school and third in the city. How did she manage it? She guessed. 'I resigned myself to failure,' she said afterwards, 'and decided to go ahead and guess at the answers. As I was guessing I realized I could just tell which was the right answer out of the three or four possibilities. I felt good and relaxed after I got into the test and decided to give up trying to figure out the answers. I had been extremely tense and sweating profusely. I relaxed, felt my stomach muscles unknot, and felt almost giddy with laughter.' As a result of this experience, this student learnt the value of relaxing and 'guessing'. She realized that, when she didn't know an answer to a question, or what decision to make, she could 'just let go, relax, and let the right answer for what I ought to do or decide come to me'. She acknowledges that her guesses are not always right – but they often are. And says that, if she ignores a 'guess' and does something more rational, 'I often get into trouble.' There is research evidence to support her intuition: decisions taken intuitively are often more satisfactory than those taken after much conscious deliberation.

NOW TRY THIS: Intelligent guessing

Consider some situation in your life where you are genuinely not sure how to proceed, or even, maybe, how to read the situation. First acknowledge what it is that you don't know. Then invite your unconscious to send you up a guess. Take the guess seriously. Ask yourself whether there might be some truth to it. Check it out. You will not always be right by any manner of means. But get a feel for when your guesses might be more 'wise' than you might think. Cultivate an interest in the crazy stuff that your unconscious can come up with, if you let it. Learn to treat it with a mixture of amusement and respect.

Hunches

A hunch is a sense of direction – what it might be profitable to do, or how things are going to turn out. The fireman who withdrew his men from a building that was about to collapse had a hunch. The nurse who started a baby on a course of antibiotics without knowing why had a hunch. Most people have hunches. When a hunch is right, we might just have been lucky: it was a statistical fluke rather than a real premonition. But in the midst of this, there are definitely hunches that are telling us something that the unconscious is working on, but is not yet able to present directly to consciousness in an acceptable fashion. Hunches are not necessarily correct – they issue, after all, from a provisional sense of things that may always be changed in the light of subsequent events or further 'research' by the unconscious. But they are valid, and worthy of note. In situations in which you cannot know for sure how to proceed, a hunch may be the best guide you are going to get.

When operating out beyond the safe limits of routine knowledge and competence, a doctor, a parent, a musician or a navigator is all the smarter for being able to tune in to their hunches, and treat them with sceptical respect.

British general medical practitioner Chris Tibbott, like most doctors, relies on his hunches all the time. He summed up a general feeling when he said: 'I get feelings about patients even before they speak. Frequently my gut feeling has been that a patient is seriously ill – even though an examination has not revealed anything – and I have admitted them to hospital as an emergency anyway. Occasionally I have been wrong – but I've also often been thankful I reacted to the feeling that something was not right.' Charles Brook is Professor of Paediatric Endocrinology at London's University College Hospital. He trains his medical students to heed and respect their 'inner knowledge', particularly when forming a diagnosis. Says Brook: 'I go on my instincts, informed by experience, and that's certainly what I advise my students to do. Any doctor who considers himself a good clinician – which means someone who gets it right most of the time – would not rule out intuition.' There are doctors who say: 'If there's nothing wrong with the test results, the patient must be OK.' Brook, like Chris Tibbott, says: 'I'm more likely to say that the test is wrong.'

Imagine you are a volunteer in an experiment on hunches. You are presented with four packs of cards, face down. You are told that on the reverse side of each card is depicted a sum of money, with a plus or minus sign. You are given a notional $2,000 stake to start with, and your job is to increase your stake as much as you can by choosing, on each 'go', one of the packs from which you will turn over the top card. Your stake goes up or down by the amount specified. What you don't know is that two of the packs, say A and C, are better bets than B and D. In B and D you get some large wins, but these are more than offset by your cumulative losses. In A and C, your wins are smaller, but over time you win more consistently.

You are wired up to a device that measures the electrical conductivity of your skin – a widely used method of checking your level of arousal. And on each go you are asked to say why you are choosing that particular pile, and how confident you feel. At first, you haven't a clue what is going on and you choose at random. Then you still think you are guessing, but your skin conductance begins to differentiate, as you are considering your choice, between the 'good' and the 'bad' piles. Then there is a phase when you begin to get a hunch or a 'feeling' about the two bad piles, and your choices become smarter. You home in on A and C, but you can't say why. Eventually, you are able to articulate what the difference between the two pairs of packs is, and to rationalize your choices.

When American neurologist Antonio Damasio gives this test to people who have damage to a certain part of the frontal lobes of their brains, they behave in a surprising way. Like you, they are eventually able to explain what is going on – and over about the same period of time. They develop an accurate, conscious understanding of the different constitutions of the four packs of cards. But they never get better at making their choices. Despite their understanding, they continue to behave 'stupidly'. Their skin conductivity never comes to differentiate between the packs, and they do not experience any hunches. It is as if their cleverness has become detached from their real-life intelligence: their ability to make smart choices. Damasio argues that, far from being an inferior kind of knowledge, intuition actually forms the vital bodily glue that holds the different bits of our intelligence together. Without the ability to hear, heed, respect and act on our hunches, we become the ultimate 'articulate incompetents'.

Inklings

There are two parts to an 'inkling'. They may emerge together, or one may come ahead of the other. One is a vague, shadowy sense of a whole; something that feels obscurely relevant to a problem, or an idea that you might want to express, like an out-of-focus image that feels meaningful but its meaning is not yet clear. The other is a luminous detail: a small vignette, an image from a dream, or a snatch of an overheard conversation that seems to glow with vague potential. Intuitions often first emerge as such a germ or the seed of an idea. A hazy sense of a solution to a problem, or of the focus of a new project, starts to crystallize around a particular fragment of experience, but you don't yet know why, or what form the 'finished product' is going to take.

An inkling is a subtle sense of something, often with no evidence to back it up. It is even quieter than the other voices of intuition we have been exploring and yet can sometimes be more powerful. We have an inkling that what we are being told does not quite ring true and we sometimes need the courage to explore it a bit further. Often they can help us to make better choices earlier than we would otherwise have done.

Creative people learn how not to squash their inklings out of hand, but rather to give them a little space to grow and be heeded from time to time.

■ Being flexible in your thinking

As we have been stressing throughout this book, creative people know that it is smart to be flexible. They are able to draw on different mental skills, and engage different states of awareness, at different times, as appropriate. Sometimes they may do this self-consciously. But mostly it just happens.

Interestingly, creative people show different patterns of brain activity depending on what phase of a problem they are working on. Colin Martindale from the University of Maine attached small sensors to people's heads while they were doing a task and recorded the level of their EEG, a measure of how aroused people are, and the state of integration of their brainwaves. First Martindale took a baseline reading of their EEG when they were just sitting relaxed, and then he asked them to work on a two-stage task. In the first stage, they were asked to think up a children's bedtime story, and in the second, to work on the storyline, refining and elaborating it and putting it into a more systematic shape.

His subjects were divided into those who scored highly on a general test of creativity and those whose scores were much lower. On the second part of the task, where people needed to be in a more focused, methodical, analytical frame of mind, the EEG patterns of the two groups showed no difference. For both, their level of cortical arousal was significantly higher than baseline. This is what you would expect. High arousal corresponds to more focused attention.

However on the first, 'creative' part of the task, where they had to allow the basic idea for the story to come 'from nowhere', the more creative subjects showed EEG levels that were actually lower than their baseline readings. They had moved into quite a different mode, in which their brainwaves were defocused and soft. The 'uncreative' subjects, however, showed the same raised level of arousal that they used (appropriately) in the elaboration phase of the task. They had forgotten how to separate being clever from being creative, and had lost the vital flexibility that the creative subjects had retained.

Everyone can develop their intuition

By now, we hope that you are beginning to see your intuition in a new light. No longer something to be disregarded as second rate, your intuition is beginning to take its place alongside your analytical judgement as a useful way of making sense of the world in many circumstances. Above all, it can be nurtured and developed to help you become better at heeding your inner voices.

In the next chapter we will find more about the best ways in which the promptings of your intuition can be harvested. We will continue with our exploration of the *orientation* dimension and dig deeper into the well of your creative memories to see how you can begin to access what you *already* know.

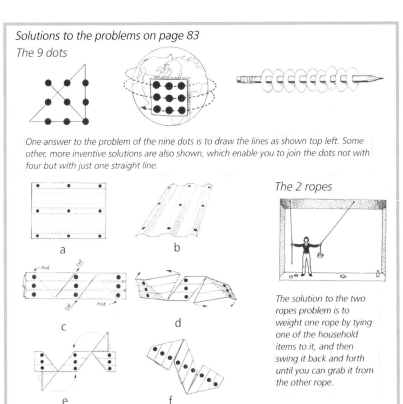

Solutions to the problems on page 83
The 9 dots

One answer to the problem of the nine dots is to draw the lines as shown top left. Some other, more inventive solutions are also shown, which enable you to join the dots not with four but with just one straight line.

a

b

c

d

e

f

The 2 ropes

The solution to the two ropes problem is to weight one rope by tying one of the household items to it, and then swing it back and forth until you can grab it from the other rope.

'We know much more than we know we know'

Michael Polanyi, philosopher

Chapter 4
Looking inward: how to use your creative memory

○ Surfing your inner-net

○ Understanding resonance

○ Developing active imagining

○ Using your habit map

'Memory is the diary that we all carry about with us.'

Oscar Wilde

Being creative means making the best use of what you already know, to help you meet new and unusual challenges. In the last chapter our orientation shifted and we began to turn inwards. Now we will do this in earnest, exploring the different ways in which we can access the multifaceted and multimedia 'diary' that we all carry around with us. For creativity, we might say, is essentially about optimizing the contact between the present and the past, between perception and memory, between the predicament we see ourselves as being in now and the stored inner resources we can call upon to respond. So we need as good an understanding as we can get of what memory is, how it is organized, and how its lost archives can best be found and read. And the best 'image' we can use for memory is that of the brain itself.

How can a lump of spongy meat give rise to anything so subtle and sophisticated as human creativity: to Michelangelo's David or Einstein's Theory of Relativity? It seems impossible. But let's take a closer look. There is nothing inside the human head but blood and bone, fluids and tissues, muscles and tubes, and most importantly nerve cells, or 'neurons'. These small bushy filaments, like miniature trees, sum together the tiny electrical tingles that impinge on their roots and, if the sum is big enough, distribute another shower of tingles to their neighbours' roots via their own branches. Experience alters the receptivity of each root-tip to its adjacent branches: that is how learning takes place, and how memories are laid down. As experience cumulatively makes some of the junctions easier for the 'spark' to leap across, and others harder, so functional grooves are worn in the brain that channel the flow of its activity. All our impressions, habits and flights of fancy are represented in the brain by these patterns of neural connections, and by the ways in which they direct the electrical charges that continually run through them.

In essence, that's what brains are, and how they work. There are no libraries, no librarians and no indexes in the head; no spreadsheets or microchips; no tape recorders; no dictionaries. There are no boxes labelled 'short-term memory' and 'long-term memory', and no cinema screen on which the contents of memory can be displayed to consciousness, or across which trains of thought travel like tickertape. And, as far as we know, there is no real muse that whispers insights or premonitions in your ear while you are asleep. These are all just metaphors: images that some brains have come up with to try to capture something of the way they work. The more we know about how the brain actually works, the less we need these more fanciful analogies.

■ The three layers of memory

It seems that the brain is organized into three 'layers'. The most basic layer is laid down by our genes before we are born. Just as our bodies are genetically shaped in the womb into arms and legs, liver and lungs and so on, so our evolutionary history is also hard-wired into the brain's structure and function. Vision is located at the back of the brain, the mechanisms that control our level of arousal are buried in the middle, while those that have fine control over the focus of our attention are at the front. We are pre-set to find human faces attractive; to associate an angry voice with an angry expression; to learn a language. We 'know' about gravity, and the limitations it places on our movement. And we may also 'know', in a similar sense, about some of the great themes that run through human lives: the archetypal stories of tragedy and trickery, heroism and romance, the wisdom of the elders, the renewing powers of nature and the perfidy of lovers. We may not know that we know them, yet somehow all cultures seem to respond to them, recognize them and symbolize them in their art and their mythology.

Carl Jung suggested that such grand, recurrent themes are latent in our brains, in the same way as our physical responses to injury or illness are latent in our immune systems. It is these deep, universal tendencies of the human brain to pattern our experience in certain ways that he referred to individually as the 'archetypes', and all together as 'the collective unconscious'. People have sometimes mistakenly taken the collective unconscious to refer to some kind of disembodied, ethereal pool of memory, somewhere 'out there', into which the more sensitive of us can tap; but Jung was clear that he was talking about something straightforwardly biological. Call this the first layer of organization.

Layer 1: the archetypal layer

Our individual experiences are overlaid on this pre-contoured landscape and form the second layer. In every moment there is a unique, ephemeral configuration of activation in the brain, and all the neurons that are simultaneously active are briefly bound together into a pattern that persists, however faintly, as a 'memory'. Every moment, though we may not be aware of it, we are adding to this vast archive of autobiographical snapshots and episodes. Some of these records may have passed through conscious awareness on their way in, but many will have been registered subliminally, or have become inaccessible with the passage of time.

Layer 2: the inner-net

Let us call this layer of memory the 'inner-net'. It is rich, detailed, and relatively unorganized and unsystematic. And it is of no more use in routine, daily life, than the box of treasured memorabilia under the bed. What we need, to get through the day, is the third layer, which we call the 'habit map'.

Layer 3: the habit map

As the records of the inner-net accumulate, so repeated patterns emerge, just as they would if you were to pile up a stack of slides of nearly identical scenes and look through them all at once. These recurrent elements of experience come to wear into the neural landscape a network of channels that are broader, deeper and more persistent than any individual memory. And these 'concepts' and 'habits' are themselves organized into familiar 'scripts' or 'scenarios'. We just know, without thinking about it, what to expect and how to behave when we have dinner in a restaurant, as opposed to at a friend's house. You do not, unless you are being funny, tip your hostess, nor do you offer to help the waiter with the washing up. This level of knowledge enables us to function smoothly, effectively and efficiently while the world continues to run on familiar lines.

The development of the habit map does not, however, wipe the traces of the inner-net – and for good reason. If it did, we would be lost whenever the world behaved unpredictably. We would be stuck with our habits, and no quick way to get out of them. We would have no basis on which to have second thoughts, or from which to construct a novel response to novel events. We could slowly learn to adapt – if we were not wiped out in the meantime. But we would not be able to be creative. Though, under normal circumstances, the faint filigree of the inner-net is hard to see behind the much clearer and firmer markings of the habit map, when we need to, we might be able to go back to it and think again. But just as we can only see the stars at night when the sun has gone down, though they are there all the time, so we can only gain access to the inner-net when we quieten down the familiar voices and directions of the habit map.

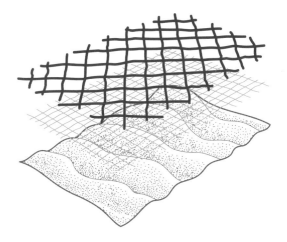

So the brain becomes effectively organized into layers that shade into each other. Most easily accessible is the habit map: the patterns that are most well entrenched and easiest to articulate. It is these well-marked channels of concept, talk and expectation that drive perception when we are in top-down, diagnostic mode. We see in terms of the coarsest, most stereotyped patterns we possess, and much of the time it is (as we have seen) fast and efficient to do so. Narrow-focus attention picks out the most well-defined grooves that have been etched into the surface of the mind.

Layers of awareness and types of focus

But these patterns are the most conventional and the most well segmented. It is as if what one sees on the surface is a political map of the mind's contents, with different countries apparently clearly demarcated and marked in different colours. Such a map invites you to think and talk in certain ways, but effectively conceals more fine-grain, less systematic interconnections. If you are going to see and think 'creatively', you need to go below these categories and explore the territory of memory in more detail. There may be other patterns – rivers and mountain ranges – that meander and cut across the more obvious boundaries between 'countries': patterns that are more personal and idiosyncratic on the one hand, or more deeply collective and universal on the other.

- And for this you need the more detailed and holistic gaze of *soft-focus attention*. You need to be able to look inwards on your own landscape of memory with the same patient, receptive attitude that we explored, looking outwards, in Chapter 2. And this is the state of awareness that we earlier referred to as 'intuitive'. This is the mood within which new patterns, remote analogies and associations, and the telling detail, may become visible to the mind's eye.
- *In tight-focus mode*, the mind behaves like a well-organized desk with many drawers, each of which contains a compendium of knowledge, skills and concepts for dealing with a particular kind of scenario.
- *In broad-focus mode*, the mind behaves like a giant spider's web of interconnected ideas and experiences, which reverberates widely whenever it is touched at a particular point.

There is a real sense in which we see what we want to see. As psychologist Kurt Koffka put it: 'We see things not as they are, but as we are.' But you do not need to rely on psychologists to know that there is far more going on beneath the surface than at first meets the eye. Already in this book, we have seen many examples of significant thoughts and feelings which lie beneath the surface of our conscious minds. If you want to find out more about how to access your creative self, you will want to access these on a more regular basis than you currently do. We call this 'surfing your inner-net'.

We know that, even before information is served up to us consciously, the brain has been hard at work. It has been organizing our experiences in terms of our hopes, fears, habits and expectations before we have 'woken up' to what is going on. We become consciously aware of things only after much of what we know, believe and want has already been dissolved in our perception.

We can get smarter if we learn how to manage this behind-the-scenes activity more skilfully and flexibly. Just as our frame of mind influences the kind of data we pick up, so too does it affect the kind of resonance that data has with the accumulated wisdom (or otherwise) of our memory store.

NOW TRY THIS: Reliving versus recollecting

It is possible to get a feel for the difference between the habit map and the inner-net by trying to access your own memory in one or other of the two modes of awareness.

First, try the deliberate, hard-focus mode. Remember a classroom that you used when you were about 14 or 15 years old. Just see what comes to mind when you try to recall it 'cold' in this way. Can you recall the name of the teacher who taught you in that room? Any of the names of your classmates? Give it a few moments to see what comes up. You may not be able to recall very much.

OK, now try it in soft-focus mode. Get someone to talk you through the following instructions. Or, if you are on your own, read through the instructions first and then follow them from memory. First, do your relaxation exercise. Close your eyes, take the three deep breaths, let out your sighs, lean back, and allow your body and mind to go into their soft, relaxed inward state. Now let an image of the classroom come to mind. Let your imagination build the image of the classroom as fully as possible. See if you can relive the experience of being in that classroom as fully as possible. Feel that you are really back there.

Look around (in your mind's eye). Where are the windows? What shape are they? What can you see outside? What is the weather like? If there is any sunlight, notice the patterns it makes in the room. Can you feel the temperature? Do you feel warm or cold? Notice the door into the room. What sort of door is it? If there is glass in it, what can you see through it? How is the room laid out? Notice the blackboards, the teacher's desk, and any other paraphernalia at the front of the room.

Now be aware of where you are sitting in the room. Look around at the other people. Is there anyone sitting in front of you? What does the back of their head look like? Who is sitting next to you? What are they wearing? How do you feel about this person? Notice where the other people are sitting who are significant to you in some way… Where are your friends sitting? What are their names? What about people you may be scared of, or dislike? Who are they? How do you feel about them? What does it feel like to be you at that age?

Now notice the teacher at the front of the room. How do you feel towards them? What is your mood? Are you interested and engaged with the lesson, or preoccupied and withdrawn? Do you feel rebellious? Do you want the teacher's approval? What else is on your mind?

OK, how was that? Were you able to relive it? Did you find yourself spontaneously filling in more details than you thought you knew? Did some names pop into your mind that you had not thought about for years? Were you able to 'be' the adolescent that you actually were?

Many people, when they do an exercise like this, are astounded by how much they are able to remember. Were you able to feel the difference between the rather pale abstractions that 'recollecting' tends to come up with, and the rich, detailed memories that come when you 'relive' an experience? That's the difference between accessing the habit map and gently surfing the inner-net.

Developing resonance

Being creative requires the ability to look outwards in a way that allows the situation to tell you as much as it can, being open to its unique constellation of information and to alternative ways of putting this information together, at the same time as remaining sensitive to the subtler, fainter and richer layers of information stored in your inner-net. And often, of course, it requires the ability to do these two things together, so that a rich picture of the 'predicament' is able to resonate with the rich resources of the inner-net. This is what we mean by 'resonance', slowly looking outwards from deep within yourself.

If you have ever gone through the process of moving house, you may have had this kind of experience. Such a decision involves some hard facts – how much the house costs and how far it is from your work, for example, but much of the information you are seeking to process is much more subtle and likely to be stored on your inner-net. How do you feel when you walk in? Does the neighbourhood feel right? What is the potential of the place? Can you imagine yourself in the space? What memories of earlier houses, perhaps even childhood homes, does it evoke?

This idea of resonance between problem (the things that you perceive which have led you to describe something as a 'problem') and database (your inner-net and all its store of memories) is, perhaps, the most important of all the keys to creativity. In normal perception, especially in hard-focus mode, this resonance happens so fast that we are not aware of it. In the blink of an eye, the scene settles into an interpretation based on the categories of the habit map. But in creativity, this resonance is slowed down and drawn out, so that we are aware of a more prolonged search for meaning or resolution. It involves a kind of thinking which is not directed, not busy, not purposeful and not clear – because all those attitudes orientate you towards the more superficial layers of the mind. Many people would not even count it as 'thinking' at all, for it seems hazy, haphazard and uncontrolled. Yet it is the state of mind within which perception and memory can talk to each other in a way that allows each to be transformed by the delicate, open-minded promptings of the other. It is the state within which ideas and perceptions that are both novel *and* appropriate to a problem can emerge.

Case Study

At a seminar we conducted for members of the Innovation Exchange at the London Business School on 'intuition in business decision-making', we spent some time talking about some of the ideas we have been discussing here. During the break, a senior executive from British Telecom started talking about his experience solving jigsaw puzzles. He liked to unwind at the end of the day by spending half an hour or so with his on-going puzzle – usually something fiendishly difficult with about 5000 pieces. He told us that he had discovered he could go about it in two ways. He could pick a likely-looking piece and carefully inspect the half-finished puzzle to see if it would fit anywhere. Doing it this way, he reckoned to fit about six pieces or so in the 30 minutes. But he had found that he could also hold a piece in his hand and gaze at the puzzle in a much more unfocused way, waiting for the rightful place to pop out at him. And if he adopted this strategy, he could do about twice as many pieces. 'Is that the kind of thing you're on about?' he asked tentatively. 'Yes,' we told him. 'That's exactly it.' And he had provided us with a very clear example of resonance at work.

The art of detection

A more 'professional' example of resonance at work (or 'play') is the art of detection. Good detectives are people who can look at a crime scene and see patterns of significance and meaningful details that have escaped others. This ability is often made great play of in detective fiction. The great detectives like Sherlock Holmes possess an enormous fund of experience. They immerse themselves in the details of the crime in a way that allows them to be puzzled or confused for a while. (Think of Columbo bumbling around with a distracted air as if saying to himself, 'There's something fishy here but I can't quite put my finger on it.')

And then they often withdraw into a kind of reverie in which you can almost feel the resonance process going on. Holmes retires with his pipe and commands Watson to protect him from all distractions. Morse puts his feet up and drifts away to the sound of his beloved Verdi. And then – as if by magic – it all 'falls into place'. Fictional prototypes these may be, but real and very successful detectives also exhibit many of the same characteristics. Real detectives are now taught various techniques to encourage them to notice minor clues and incidental details. And you have already met the real-life Micki Pistorius on page 48.

The process of resonance often seems to home in on the odd detail that turns out to be pregnant with meaning. Ruth Rendell's Chief Inspector Wexford solves a murder mystery by noting the different shapes of two ankles. Sherlock Holmes famously sees the vital significance of the dog that did not bark. And Sigmund Freud, himself a fan of the Conan Doyle stories, observes that: 'His method of inquiry is closely related to the technique of psychoanalysis. It, too, is accustomed to divine secret and concealed things from unconsidered or unnoticed details, from the rubbish heap, as it were, of our observations.'

■ Using images as memory triggers

'The words or the language as they are written or spoken do not seem to play any role in my mechanism of thought. The physical entities which seem to serve as elements of thoughts are certain signs and more or less clear images which can be voluntarily reproduced and combined... this combinatory play seems to be *the* essential feature in productive thought.'

Albert Einstein

One of the strongest and most valuable connecting media to your inner-net is imagery. Through the medium of imagination we can access our deepest thoughts and feelings, allow our quandaries to 'sink down' and answers to 'bubble up' in ways that are more productive than rational thought can ever be. Through imagery we can gain access to the deeper layers of our experience, and allow them to interact and recombine in entertaining and productive ways.

Images have a number of useful qualities. They are more detailed and concrete than strings of words. Images preserve more of the richness of experience. And they make available memories and ideas that we do not know we have, either because they do not fit with the concepts of the habit map and so are pared away when we are in hard-focus mode, or because they were registered subliminally in the first place.

- Images are multisensory. Though we sometimes use the words 'imagination' and 'visualization' interchangeably, images often contain sounds and smells and tastes as well. When we use the word 'lemon' (as in 'Don't forget to put "lemons" on the shopping list') we know what to buy, but we don't automatically re-experience much of the lemon-ness of lemons. When we imagine a specific lemon, in all its multimedia detail, we can see its pitted skin, feel the waxy texture, smell its sharp aroma and taste its juice. When we go shopping, we do not need all this additional information. But at other times, it can be very useful. It is especially useful, sometimes, to be able to use imagination to 'taste' the physical sensations that go along with an experience: to feel what its bodily concomitances are, and to make contact with the emotional feelings that it may excite in us.

- Images present complicated information and ideas to us in a way that is more coherent and integrated. 'A picture tells us more than a thousand words' not only because it contains more detail, but because those details are bound into patterns and contained in relationships that are hard to articulate. Look up and notice the scene around you. How much of all that richness could you write down, or tell someone about over the phone? Categories like 'blue' and 'square' and 'pine' and 'behind' convey just the bare bones of our experience – bones that may pick out some aspects of what is significant, but at the cost of discarding almost all that makes each experience rich and unique. Images preserve much more of that intricate and holistic quality.

- Images are dynamic. We can invite the unconscious to run for us a little clip of a movie, and show us one way in which a scene develops, or how things might turn out. We can re-run events that went badly, and explore ways in which we could have done better. We can rehearse different ways of handling a tricky situation that might arise. And imagination can be freed from the constraints of what is 'real' or 'likely', to allow us to explore in our mind's eye situations we have never met, or interesting possibilities that might not get much air time when we are in more rational or sensible modes.

- Images are also able to offer more fertile symbols, analogies and metaphors. We use words to propose that 'memory is like a library', or 'the atom is like the solar system', and can then use our imaginations to explore the way in which the structures of relationships in the two domains map on to each other, and see what interesting questions they raise. How are our memories filed? Are they separate, like books on shelves, or more interconnected... perhaps memory is more like a spider's web. Who or what is the librarian? Because images can incorporate much more personal detail, they are capable of being more evocative, more intricate and more novel than mere words can.

Finally, imagery is able to reach down below the details of personal experience and represent some of the archetypal themes and concerns that are common to all human beings. As we enter a mood in which the inner-net is able to resonate more finely and deeply with our experience, so we may find images bubbling up that are coloured and shaped by these fundamental concerns. Through the use of imagery you may get ideas that are more deeply meaningful and which go beyond your habit map. Isabel Allende relies on her dreams to serve back up to her such small snatches of experience: 'I believe that there is another world, the world of dreams, that is like a world inside our minds where we store information that we don't know we have. During the day I overhear conversations, I see flashes, but I don't record them in conscious memory. Unconsciously, I store them inside. When I dream, I have access to that storage place where events are. I use that information, when I can remember it, when I wake up.'

Using layers of perception

Making use of the qualities of images enables us to get smarter in a variety of ways. At the simplest level, imagery enables us to call to mind more of what we know, and to 'remember' experiences that we were not conscious of the first time around. Poets and artists often rely on their imaginations to throw up poignant details from their subliminal past.

Isabel Allende relies on her dreams to serve back up to her such small snatches of experience: 'I believe that there is another world, the world of dreams, that is like a world inside our minds where we store information that we don't know we have. During the day I overhear conversations, I see flashes, but I don't record them in conscious memory. Unconsciously, I store them inside. When I dream, I have access to that storage place where events are. I use that information, when I can remember it, when I wake up.'

NOW TRY THIS: Imagining a strawberry

Here is an exercise to see how much of your detailed memory you can recreate through the use of imagination.

Close your eyes. Take your three deep breaths. Relax. Turn your attention inwards. Let your mind and your body go soft and quiet.

Now imagine you are holding a strawberry in the palm of your hand. See it resting in your hand as clearly as you can. Look at it. What shape is this specific strawberry? How big is it? See how red it is. See how the shade of red varies from place to place on the surface of the strawberry. Notice where the light strikes it. Notice where the skin is shiny and where it is duller. Notice the seeds embedded in the skin. What colour are they? How close together are they? Does your strawberry have a stalk? If so, examine the leaves. See what colour and shape they are. How many leaves are there?

Now imagine that you put the strawberry on a table and cut it in half with a knife. How does the knife feel as it goes through? Take half the strawberry and feel it. What does the outer skin feel like? Strike your finger across the cut surface… feel how different that is. Press the flesh: how soft is it? Does it bounce back, or does the imprint stay in the surface? Notice the colours and patterns on the cut surface. You might have got juice on your fingers…

how does it feel? Is it sticky? Do you like the feel? Do you want to lick your finger?

Now bring the strawberry up to your nose and smell it. Inhale its rich perfume. Lick along the outside surface. Now lick the cut surface. Compare how they taste. Take a little bite out of the outside of the strawberry. Feel the texture in your mouth. Can you feel the little seeds? Taste it. How sweet is it? Do you like the taste? Swallow it. Feel the motions of your throat as you swallow. Now take a bite out of the middle. Is it different? How? The texture? The taste? OK, now open your eyes and come back.

Even in such a simple exercise, you may be surprised how much you 'know' about strawberries: how detailed your knowledge is of the texture of the skin, what the stalk looks and feels like, and how the paler filaments in the centre look and taste. How much of this information have you ever been fully conscious of before?

Mental rehearsal

We know that creative visualizations like this are useful for athletes who are unable to train through illness but can still practise through visualization. The same is true for performers preparing for concerts and choosing to undertake detailed mental rehearsal of their pieces. There may be areas of your own life which could be improved by using this technique (other than your ability to salivate at a strawberry)!

■ Seeing other worlds

Imagination enables you to break free from your normal perspective, and even from the 'real world', and see how things look, or might look, from other perspectives, and on the basis of different assumptions. When average school students were asked to imagine being a very good student, they were able to produce better work than they normally did. They were able to empathize with the way good students saw the task of writing an essay, and 'knew' how to do it.

Case Study

The ability to synthesize novel images is of practical value. The Chinese research chemist Yuan Tseh Lee won the Nobel Prize in 1986 for explaining how complex molecules interact with each other during certain kinds of chemical reactions. His fundamental insights came to him when he was actively trying to imagine what it would be like to be one of these molecules. He even found it helped if he endowed them with human-like motives and feelings. In a lecture to a conference of chemistry educators in Australia, ten years later, he argued strongly that we should be teaching science students how to make better use of their imaginations.

NOW TRY THIS: Imagining things you've never experienced

Go into your relaxed inner state. Close your eyes. Now imagine your strawberry again (or it could be a new one). See it clearly. Now take it to your dream house. Sit outside your dream house. Place the strawberry in front of you. Let the strawberry start to get bigger. Let it grow and grow and grow in size. See how its skin looks now. Feel how much smaller you are relative to the strawberry. Now let it grow until it is out higher than the roof of your house. Let it grow till it is about 100 feet tall.

Climb inside the strawberry at the bottom. Start crawling upwards through the strawberry. Notice what the quality of the light is like in there. Is the flesh of the strawberry pressing on your body? How does it feel? Is it nice or not? Do you want to eat some of the fruit as you go? Go ahead. Now climb right to the peak of the strawberry and climb out of the top. As you look around, you see people sitting on the top of giant strawberries as far as the eye can see. They are all waving to each other. Wave back. Everyone is covered in sticky strawberry goo. They all look happy. Slide down the outside of your strawberry gently to the ground. Clap your hands and make all the strawberries disappear.

Now go into your dream house. Look out of the window at the lake. Dive in. Feel the cool water on your skin. Splash around. Get all the sticky goo off you. Dive down. You meet a shoal of beautiful small fish. See their colours. Breathe them in so they are swimming around in your chest. How does that feel? Let them swim through your lungs into your blood and swim around your body. Feel these bright, beautiful flecks of fish swimming into every part of you. Feel them in your toes. In your heart. Open your mouth and breathe them out in a continuous stream. Come back up to the surface of the lake.

Now go back into your dream house where you can be dry and warm. Sit comfortably and relax. Feel your body just as it 'really' is. It's time to say goodbye to the house and come back to the present.

■ Controlling your imagination

In the last few years of the nineteenth century, a Serbian-American inventor named Nikola Tesla was laying the foundations for the electrical technology that was to drive the twentieth century. He was the originator of alternating-current motors and generators, and it was Tesla, not Marconi, who invented the radio. He was also the father of modern-day robotics.

Case Study

From an early age, Tesla was able to imagine the workings of machines in three dimensions, and in remarkable detail, and he used this ability not just to construct his inventions but also to run them for long periods to see where they might break down or wear out. Tesla said of this extraordinary gift for imagery:

'It is absolutely immaterial to me whether I run my turbine in thought or test it in my shop. I even note if it is out of balance. In this way I am able to rapidly develop and perfect a conception without touching anything. When I have gone so far as to embody in the invention every possible improvement I can think of and see no fault anywhere, I put into concrete form this final product of my brain. Invariably my device works as I conceived that it should, and the experiment comes out exactly as I planned it. In twenty years there has not been a single exception.'

Not all of us are as adept at controlled imagery as Nikola Tesla. But all of us could be better at it than we are. Just like writing or logical thinking, it is a skill that can be developed, not a God-given talent. If we are facing a difficult meeting, we can run it in the imagination, and by doing so prepare ourselves for the feelings or frustrations that might emerge (and so be less thrown by them if they do occur), and try out a variety of approaches to see which 'feels right'. Students coming up to an examination do better if they have spent just a few minutes each day imagining the process of revision.

Practising physical skills in imagination has also been shown to be beneficial. People who spent ten minutes a day imagining themselves throwing darts at a board improved their accuracy on a final test by 22 per cent. Preparing to undertake a skilful action also benefits from a rehearsal in imagination. Golfer Jack Nicklaus said that before every shot, he 'went to the movies inside his head', imagining first the position of the ball after the shot, then the trajectory it would have to take to get there, and finally the feel of the swing that would set the ball off on that trajectory. 'These home movies are a key to my concentration and to my positive approach to every shot,' he said.

There are some important lessons from these examples.

- First, imagination works better if you are inside your skin, in the image, rather than looking on from a 'third person' perspective. When you are imagining from the inside, your image includes the bodily feelings, both emotional and kinaesthetic, which go along with the scene, and these turn out often to be crucial.
- Secondly, it works much better to imagine the process than the product. If Jack Nicklaus had *only* imagined the ball where he wanted it to be, his home movie would not have worked. Students who just imagined themselves having done well in the exam, and not the process of revision, did less well in the actual examination even than a group who did no visualization at all.
- And finally, and most obviously, you can't use your imagination successfully if you don't have a good body of experience on which to base your imagination. Imagination works with the database it has got, and if that is thin, the imagery it can produce will be coarse. Perhaps that is why groups who do best in these studies are often those who

combine both imaginary and physical practice. Imagination draws the best out of the experience you have, and further experience tests out and refines the products of imagination.

Active imagining

The quality of imagination varies depending on the mood in which we use it, and the purpose to which it is put. In the sections above we have been talking about forms of imagery that are actively controlled and directed. There is a clear goal – to prepare for a meeting, or improve a golf shot – and the process of imagination is actively managed. Under these circumstances, you get a more narrow-focus kind of imagery that is good for fine-tuning. It gets you into the detail of the inner-net, but does not put it into its most resonant and creative state. For that you need the more dreamy kind of reverie that we talked about earlier. But before we return to reverie, here is an exercise that is a kind of halfway house. The imagery is directed, but you are coming at a problem in a sideways, symbolic way that may allow for greater creativity.

NOW TRY THIS: **Journey to a solution**

The first stage in this exercise is to formulate a problem or a question that currently concerns you, but which you feel stuck or blocked about. Choose one of those from your deep awareness exercise on pages 35–7, if you like. Make it a middle-sized problem, nothing too trivial or too momentous. Get the question as clear in your mind as you can. Let it sink into your mind.

- Now turn inward. Do your relaxation exercise, close your eyes and allow the problem to drift below the horizon of your mind. It is still there, but not in your conscious awareness. You might like to feel that the problem is gently colouring your conscious mind, like a pale sunset. Let your mind go quiet and calm.

- Now imagine you are on the shore of your lake, in front of your dream house. It is a warm afternoon. You climb into a small boat and push off into the lake. Lie in the bottom of the boat in the sunshine with your eyes closed, listening to the lapping of the water and feeling the gentle rocking as you drift along. The boat is being carried along by a current that will take you where you need to go. You are quite safe. Just relax.

- You notice that the light is fading and you see that you have drifted into an underground passage. It gets darker and darker, but you continue to drift along relaxed and peaceful… Then the boat comes out into the light again, and you find yourself in a beautiful quiet sunlit meadow. The boat drifts to the bank and you step out into the meadow. In this place someone or something will bring you a message. The message may or may not seem relevant to the question you posed at the beginning. It may not even seem to make sense.

- Allow yourself to receive the message, and trust that all will become clear. Be quiet and still in the meadow, and wait for the messenger to bring something to you. It may be in words; it may be an image; it may be an object; it may be a mixture of things…

- When you have experienced whatever it is that you came to the meadow for, get back into the boat and drift away. Very quickly you will find yourself back on the shore of the lake in front of your house. Go up into the house and lie down quietly. Recall your message and reflect on it. Let the message and the problem gently talk to each other. See what they have to say to each other. See if the message suggests a way forward for you.

- When you are ready, come back to the present and open your eyes. You may want to take a moment to record your message in your 'waking mind' in some way.

Frances Vaughan, from whose book *Awakening Intuition* this exercise is adapted, tells of a woman who did this exercise when she was struggling with the question of whether to get pregnant. In the meadow she became a mother with a newborn baby. The image was so clear, and she felt such a powerful, unequivocal love for the baby, and a sense of 'rightness' to the scene, that she knew for certain that she wanted to have a child – despite all the doubts and misgivings that had been buzzing around in her head.

Daydreaming

Active, controlled imagining is good for learning and problem solving. But for real creativity you need to use your imagination in a way that is slower and more receptive. Daydreaming is very good for this.

Case Study

Trevor Bayliss is a prolific and successful British inventor. His most famous device is the clockwork radio – an occasional fashion accessory in the West, and a prodigious life-saver in Africa. Bayliss got the idea from a daydream. He explains: 'I was watching a television programme about the spread of AIDS in Africa… these kids lying on rush mats, covered in flies, and they said education was the only way to help people. But how to get the message across? For some reason I started to imagine myself like General Bayliss, you know, gin and tonic in hand, monocle and this wind-up gramophone playing Nelly Melba. I realized that if a wind-up could drag a rusty needle round a record…' He has since gone on to develop a clockwork laptop computer, a new water purification system (using the same power source as the radio), a land-mine detector and, most recently, a geostationary tracking device.

Dreams

Dreams are imaginary stories that bubble up from the depths of the inner-net. Sometimes they seem straightforward and rather matter-of-fact. Sometimes they are fragmentary: just bits and pieces of flotsam from the unconscious that don't seem to have any meaning or relevance to anything. Not all dreams are pregnant with significance. But some are. In particular, watch out for dreams that seem to integrate details of your life with the deeper, archetypal themes that lie at the bottom of your mind. They may be involuntary reminders of themes or concerns that are being excluded from the more purposeful, disciplined thoughts of waking consciousness. We can use dreams to draw our attention to questions and concerns that may have become excluded from the habit map.

In dreams we can look at ourselves with greater honesty, and in greater depth. Sometimes a dream will be showing us something that is neglected or in need of repair. Dream expert Montague Ullman suggests that dreams are telling us about what is ruptured or unresolved in our relationships with others.

In dreams, three things happen:

- We surf the inner-net for these neglected problems.
- We can uncover coping mechanisms and responses that may have been of use in analogous situations.
- The wide, shallow spread of activity through the inner-net enables us to find more remote connections than we could in deliberate problem-solving mode.

Because these associations are diverse and diffuse, the only way they have to make themselves known to consciousness is through analogies and symbols that may, on first sight, seem bizarre or nonsensical. Though we are not able to predict the form of a particular dream, the approach we have been developing here certainly enables us to understand the general shape of them.

We are built to be alert to threats to our survival and our well-being. Sources of danger need to be attended to. Just as a cat becomes instantly awake and focused in the presence of an unfamiliar noise, so it was with our ancestors who paid attention to whatever was in need of maintenance and repair. Those who did not were less likely to survive. Some of these threats are physical and some social. Some come from the outside and some from within. Some are immediate and some linger from the past. A cat licks a wound he received in a fight to keep it clean and aid its healing. Well-off human beings are subject more often to threats of the social than the physical type, and those that are not 'licked' and mended may fester. It is against our evolutionary nature to ignore them. Consciously we may forget how vital this connective tissue is and allow its tears to remain as we busily pursue our personal agendas. Some of our dreams call our attention to those necessary repairs that we may be in danger of neglecting.

How are we best to heed these calls from within?

- The first thing is to stay away from books that purport to offer specific interpretations of dream events or to provide a 'dictionary' of symbols, with the aid of which one can construct a definitive interpretation. Even Freud did not believe that trains and snakes always meant penises, or that wells and tunnels were vaginas. Jung said: 'No dream symbol can be separated from the individual who dreams it, and there is no definite or straightforward interpretation of any dream.' If you want to make a party game out of dream interpretation, that's fine; but it has nothing to do with getting smarter. Each dream derives its meaning from the whole context of your life – past and present, as well as hopes and fears for the future – and it is not to be dissected and labelled according to some anatomy textbook.

● Secondly, do not be too mystical about dreams. They do not come with a certificate guaranteeing their profundity. Just as many stray images and intuitions are not worth pondering, so are many dreams. Some dreams are worth spending time with, and the more you get to know your dream life, the better you will be able to tell which those are. For instance, the useful ones often have a particular feeling tone. Their mood is anxious, or inquisitive, or revolting, or joyous, or violent. The presence of such a tone usually gives you a clue as to which dreams are trying to tell you something, and even a first tentative idea what they may be about.

● Thirdly, learning to capture your dreams, so that you can hold them still and get to know them, is certainly useful. You need to be alert and gentle in approaching them, just like a butterfly collector has to wait and watch patiently for a specimen to appear, and then wield the net both quickly and softly so as to capture the butterfly securely but without damaging its wings.

The best way to get hold of your dreams is to cultivate the habit of 'waking before you wake'. You open up one corner of your mind which is already quite alert and watchful before the rest of your thoughts have been marshalled into full waking mode. You allow most of your mind to stay soft and fuzzy while being somewhat alert to what the soft and fuzzy bit is doing. In this mood of slow re-entry into the waking world, the tails of your dreams may be visible, and if you pull on them very gently, you may be able to coax the body of the dream back into your consciousness, where you can hold it still and have a look at it. Practise this morning reverie for a little while, and even people who claim to dream rarely or never may begin to catch glimpses of their night-time images.

Laboratory studies have shown that all of us do dream more than we think, and that, if we are woken in the middle of a period of so-called 'rapid eye movement sleep', we will often be able to report a dream that may normally have become inaccessible by the morning. (Actually, more recent research has found that we may be having more fragmentary images throughout the night, in every stage of sleep.)

If you are having real difficulty locating your dreams, you can try setting your alarm clock to go off at various points during the night. You may also be able to increase the likelihood of remembering your dreams if you tell yourself that you are going to do so before you fall asleep.

Having caught sight of a dream, you spend time getting to know it. What you should not do is immediately start trying to figure out what it means. Jungian analysts talk about 'befriending' the dream. You want to meet it on its own ground, to resonate with it, to invite it to tell you more about itself. You jump to no conclusions and demand from it no immediate sense. In your receptive mental state, you seek only to re-inhabit the dream, feeling out its imagery and its mood. Even if its content is weird or emotionally intense, you try to maintain this attitude of calm curiosity, neither pushing it away in disgust, nor trying to squeeze out its significance. In this mood, the dream may begin to unfold more of its meaning, in its own time.

Having allowed the dream to return to you, retaining as much of its mystery and its incongruous detail as you can, while you are coming awake, you can do two things with it. You can record it, or you can start to unpack. It is useful to sleep with your notebook by the side of the bed, so that, when you have got hold of the dream (or such fragments as you can), you can sit up and write it down before you have to do anything else.

Getting into the habit of doing this (but bearing in mind the caution against getting too obsessional) can also encourage your dreams to come to the surface. Having recorded the dream, you can come back to it later and reflect on it some more.

Part One has focused on you as a solitary individual. You have found out about the kinds of habits to cultivate and explored two of the three dimensions of the most conducive state of mind. In Part Two, we will explore what it means to be creative in the wider social milieu of work and life.

The Creative Thinking Plan
Part Two at a glance

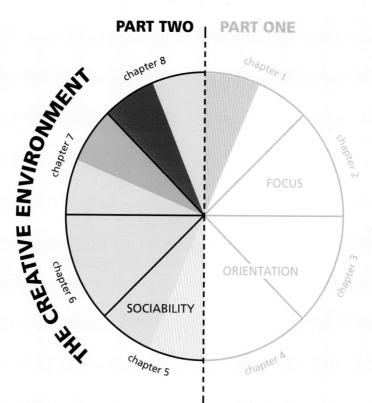

PART TWO | **PART ONE**

chapter 8

chapter 1

chapter 7

chapter 2

THE CREATIVE ENVIRONMENT

FOCUS

chapter 6

ORIENTATION

chapter 3

SOCIABILITY

chapter 5

chapter 4

KEY:

First way – Habits of mind

Second way – States of mind

Third way – Creative techniques

Fourth way – Creative contexts

PART TWO

The creative environment

Creative thought needs a mixture of sociability and solitude in order to thrive

Chapter 5
Being sociable: it's a state of mind

○ Allow time for thought and reflection

○ Keep seeking new experiences

○ Enjoy creative solitude

○ Choose creative friendships

○ Communicate your wants and needs

○ Give the bad news first

'Conversation doesn't just reshuffle the cards: it creates new cards.'

Theodore Zeldin

So far we have concentrated largely on what you as a solitary individual can do to become more creative. We have looked at the habits and frames of mind that are likely to be most conducive. But being creative involves ingeniously exploiting all the resources around you – at work and at home – and the most important of these resources are, of course, other human beings.

Even though the lifespan of a creative project may revolve around a period of solitude or a few moments of inspiration, either side of this, and interwoven with it, is an enormous amount of interaction with other people. Creativity flourishes on a mixed diet of being alone and being sociable. After *Focus* and *Orientation* comes *Sociability*, the third dimension of your state of mind. And there are many ways in which you can manage your relationships with people so that you get the best out of them and at the same time enhance your opportunities for creative development.

As we go through Part Two of *The Creative Thinking Plan* we will be exploring the creative milieu in which we all live and work and learning ways of optimizing it. Being creative involves being social in two senses. Simply through interacting with the objects of your culture – books, pictures, films, and so on – your good ideas necessarily reflect what people around you are thinking and doing, or have done and thought. And the impact that your innovations have on the world are inevitably influenced by the view of the critics, the judgement of your boss, the tastes of the book-buying public – or even the response of your children to your brilliant holiday suggestion or your radical plans for an extension to the house.

Creative people seek, and make, social climates that support and expand their ability to be creative. For example, regulating the timing, the quantity and the quality of your interactions with others is important. Constant interaction gives your mind no time to digest. Our bodies spend more time digesting than ingesting, and our minds need to do the same.

But the balance varies with both temperament and the nature of the enterprise. Writing a poem involves more solitude than rehearsing a ballet. And mathematics may require longer periods of solitary work than science. The eminent physicist and mathematician Linus Pauling, for example, said: 'Science is a very gregarious business; it's essentially the difference between having this door open and having it shut. If I'm doing 'science' [rather than mathematics], I have the door open… It's only by interacting with other people in the building that you get anything interesting done; it's essentially a communal enterprise.'

■ How personality affects creative style

Of course, everyone is an individual, with a complex set of perspectives that make us unique. We all develop different ways of doing things as we go through life. Yet, if you indulge in even the mildest form of people watching, you begin to notice that we are different in recognizably similar ways. So, Jane is funny, Malcolm is generous, Liam is grumpy, Sangeeta is charming and Britney is moody.

For example, when it comes to being quiet or being sociable, then the degree to which you are naturally outgoing or shy may have some bearing on the matter. Swiss psychiatrist Carl Jung went further than this. He developed a theory of personality that explores our preferences.

Each of these preferences describes the different ways in which you make sense of the world. Most of us are instinctively either one or the other of them, although as we get older we may well learn how to operate in the contrasting mode. As we have seen with soft and hard sensing, it is helpful to operate in one mode or the other according to the circumstances. Jung felt that we should have both alternative sets of preference in balance. (He also believed that our personality is shaped by our goals and aspirations, and that it can change throughout life. So no need to get worried that this is like having a blood-group type for life; it's not!)

Jung's thinking has been turned into one of the world's best-known tests of personality type, the Myers–Briggs Type Indicator (MBTI). For the purposes of this chapter – the degree to which being sociable is helpful to your creativity – one of these sets of preferences is especially important: extraversion and introversion. Both words come from Latin. Extraversion means 'turning out' and introversion means 'turning in' – extravert and introvert.

At first glance 'extravert' looks like 'extrovert' except that it is spelled with an 'a' in the middle (rather than the 'o' you may be used to). And there is a certain sense in which these two words are similar in meaning. Both suggest an outward focus, for example. But extrovert also carries other connotations like 'life and soul of the party' and 'always willing to make a fool of himself'. The preferences that Jung was exemplifying were about the ways in which we draw our energy in and the ways we prefer to focus our attention.

Those who are extraverted in the Jungian sense like to carry out their conversations in public. W.H. Auden's famous phrase: 'How do I know what I think until I have heard what I said?' comes to mind. Given a problem, they will want to air it in public, drawing energy from this process, like a wave draws strength from the wind and the atmosphere that surrounds it. By contrast, someone who is introverted will prefer to keep their thoughts to themselves. Faced with a tricky problem, they will want to ponder it quietly, maybe jot down a few thoughts, mull it over and return to it later. Such people are easily drained by parties and some kinds of social gatherings.

The extravert's behaviour is largely determined by objective factors. He or she is concerned with the surroundings. Jung sees extraverts as sociable, outgoing and optimistic. By contrast, the introvert's behaviour is guided more by subjective factors, with absolute standards and inner values being more important. Jung describes introverts as being less sociable, more withdrawn, more absorbed in their own inner life.

MBTI extraverts and introverts can both be shy. Both can be confident. But each has starkly different ways of drawing in energy and, therefore, of switching on their creative selves. Quiet contemplation might be a nightmare moment for an undeveloped extravert. Brainstorming can be especially tedious for an introvert. It seems that there are roughly equal numbers of extraverts and introverts spread throughout the world, although there may be some cultural differences. Understanding your own natural preference is likely to be helpful to you as you seek to develop your own creativity.

NOW TRY THIS: People watching

Take a moment to think about a number of your family members and friends. Close your eyes and let their faces 'swim' around in front of you. Concentrate on the kind of people they are rather than what they are wearing. As you think of a particular person, think about the situations in which they seem to be at their most comfortable.

Do they seem to be drawing their energy from outside or from within? Can you decide whether they are more extravert or introvert?

And what about yourself? Don't worry if you are not sure. It may be that you are just a very balanced person!

The MBTI is an excellent way of finding out more about your preferences and those of the people you live and work with, and there are many books and websites that can teach you more about it. There are many other, less well known ways too. Author Frederick L. Collins suggests the following: 'There are two types of people – those who come into a room and say, "Well, here I am!" and those who come in and say, "Ah, there you are!"'

Do you recognize the two varieties of people Collins is referring to, those who give and those who take? Which type are you? Perhaps you are both, sometimes contributing and sometimes needing to wait for others to chip in. How do you see the different kinds of people you work with? Do you find it helpful to categorize them? Or do you just generally try to get on with them?

Creative people try to avoid being overly predictable in the way they respond to given situations. At work this can be particularly important. How can you ensure that you adopt the approach that is most conducive to enhancing the creativity of you and your colleagues?

NOW TRY THIS: Colleague watching

Close your eyes and get into your relaxed state.

Think of the people you work closely with. Allow their faces to float across your mind. How does this make you feel? Think of the person you work for. What kind of person is he or she? If she or he was an animal, what would it be? What about those you work most closely with? What other images come to mind when you think about colleagues?

The way you view people really does matter. In the 1960s, drawing on research in the social sciences, management theorist Douglas McGregor famously divided people into two groups – theory X or theory Y – when it came to their attitude to work. Theory X people inherently dislike work. They prefer to be directed and respond best to tough management. Theory Y people are self-motivated. They expect to work hard for their employer. If a job is satisfying then their motivation will naturally follow. They seek responsibility and enjoy using their creativity to solve problems at work. They do not need to be driven; indeed, they don't take kindly to it. The implications of McGregor's views are clear to see. Of course, many of us have found ourselves in workplaces where theory X views hold sway.

■ Allow yourself time to think and reflect

The amount and the speed with which you communicate with other people can influence creativity either positively or negatively. Conventional wisdom, especially in the business world, says the more communication, and the more instant it is, the better. But recent research has shown that this isn't always the case. True, too little interaction is unhelpful, but so is too much. When people are in constant touch, a consensus can begin to develop too quickly around a single idea that initially looks good, and other approaches do not get a chance to be developed or heard.

It is more effective, it turns out, to intersperse periods of interaction with phases in which individuals have a chance to develop different ideas on their own. Then, when these ideas are pooled, you have a much stronger shortlist of possibilities to consider, and the approach that is eventually adopted may well be more deeply satisfactory. Here again, collective smartness depends on the rhythms and balances between different modes of operation. You may be able to recall brainstorming sessions, for example, which illustrate this tendency clearly. They may have gone well or less well and you may remember some of the elements of the chemistry of the group that contributed to this.

There is a sense in which truly creative ventures need individuals who are prepared to swim against the flow. Remember Henry Ford's remark: 'If I'd asked people what they wanted, I would have made a faster horse.'

This style of innovation in which everyone jumps to conclusions is sometimes referred to as 'Ready Fire Aim' in business (as opposed to the more logical sequencing of these three activities!). Who would have thought that people would forgo the pleasures of browsing through their local bookshop until amazon.com came along? Or that Ryanair, specialists in no-frills, low-cost air travel, would have become one of the fastest growing airlines in the world?

The power of the media is not to be underestimated, either. Especially in the early, tentative period of new thinking, the cold scorn of public scrutiny can be the last thing you need. The media wants to smooth out differences, reducing the world to black and white views of celebrity and ordinariness. The vast majority of news in the media is bad news. Indeed, when Prince Charles berated the British press for this several years ago he was roundly laughed at. But he had a point. (He must be smiling at the current growth of community newspapers whose philosophy is 'positive news'.)

Sometimes being solitary is a necessary antidote to the noise of other people's opinions. Creative people need to learn to read their own internal signals that say when it is time to go out for a walk, or sit quietly and think, or not take the daily newspapers, and just stop and be for a moment.

■ Stay conscious and seek new experiences

'New ideas come from differences. They come from having different perspectives and juxtaposing different theories.'

Nicholas Negroponte, Massachusetts Institute of Technology

Creative people relish diversity. They recognize the benefits to them of exposure to many different perspectives.

We have already touched on the way the human mind makes sense of experiences by processing and sorting them. This is an essential and important way of surviving. We have to spot patterns and file experiences or we would be forever wasting our energies. But there is a danger here. Habits rapidly become ingrained. Where once you regularly used five different routes to work depending on the circumstances, you suddenly overhear yourself defending a single option to a new colleague as if it were the only way of making the journey. Creativity requires staying open to ambiguity and possibility and not letting anyone – especially yourself – close them down.

Sometimes what we need are habit breakers, and the stimulus to these can often be found outside our own experience base or comfort zone. Creative people gratefully adapt an idea they have found in one domain and use it in a different context. Although we do not use a shopping basket to buy books when we go to the bookshop, we happily use it when we shop for books online.

Creative people get out and about. They realize that you can never know where you might find just the inspiration you need for your work or home life. Creative organizations value diversity. They make it a way of life that employees can change places from time to time. In 2000, the UK Campaign for Learning teamed up with online recruitment agency totaljobs.com to create National Job Swap Day. As a result, thousands of people have had this experience. Participants have included government ministers, CEOs of publicly listed companies, public sector leaders, teachers, receptionists, cleaners, fire fighters and many more. Indeed, in a recent survey of a thousand business people, 84 per cent said that they would like to take part in a swap and find out more about another person's job.

It seems that despite the pattern-making tendencies of our minds, which become comfortable with the way we are now, we still have a deep curiosity in other ways of doing things. Not surprisingly, those who take part in job swaps report an increase in their ability to think laterally and solve problems.

The BBC has found out that situations which force people from very different walks of life to find out about each other's lot make for very good television. In the ground-breaking BBC series, *Back to the Floor*, a chief executive changed places with a very junior employee and was exposed to what life is really like 'on the shop floor'.

The brain behind the programme was Robert Thirkell, then creative director at the BBC, who persuaded an initally sceptical senior management that this would not only be good to watch, but would also provide opportunities for people's creativity to be displayed. He was right. As a direct result of the experience of its CEO, customers at British supermarket giant Sainsbury's push smaller shopping carts. By the same token, couples getting married at Antigua's Sandals resort hear the 'Bridal March' through new remote-controlled speakers rather than through a portable CD player.

Organizations like Common Purpose in the UK and Common Cause in the USA make a virtue of exposing leaders to truly diverse experiences, believing that this will not only create better leaders, but also create a more caring and generous society. Julia Middleton, Founding CEO of Common Purpose, puts it like this: 'As professionals, we cannot afford to be isolated from our fellow decision-makers. As people, we cannot continue to be insulated from our fellow citizens. These twin beliefs are the founding principles of Common Purpose and they have continued to underpin everything we do.'

Such powerful beliefs in the value of diversity and the creative potential of experiencing a wide range of viewpoints is a strong recommendation for the kind of planned sociability you may want to explore in your life. Sixty thousand individuals in the UK have now benefited from this approach.

On the island of Jamaica, some of the local people have a wonderfully generous tradition of inviting complete strangers to join them for a meal, simply to enjoy the varied conversation that will inevitably ensue and the new insights they may gain in the process.

■ The power of creative friendship

Sometimes we just need someone to bounce our ideas off. Especially after a period when you have been working at something intensely on your own, it is good to share your emerging thoughts with someone else. Two things are important here.

- The first is that you need to be the one who decides when the moment is right for this. You need to feel your ideas are ready before you expose them to the cruel light of day.
- Secondly, it is essential that your buddy is someone you trust and respect and that you are talking to the right person for the subject you have in hand.

As co-authors and friends, we often provide each other with feedback and advice. It might be after one of us has spoken on a public platform, for example, or by looking at each other's draft thoughts on paper, or indeed, above all, through conversation.

We believe that everyone needs a buddy (or coach or mentor or critical friend; the language is different depending on which part of the world and which sector you are in). After all, we have a doctor who helps us look after our body – known as a GP or General Practitioner in the UK. Why not an LP or CP – Learning Practitioner or Creative Practitioner – to support us as we seek to become more creative?

Just think of the number of occasions when you have found a more creative solution to a problem if you have engaged someone else's experiences in helping you to solve it. In creative friendship, one plus one often adds up to many more than two.

NOW TRY THIS: A problem shared means a solution aired

Next time you are with a group of friends or colleagues, try this approach.

Take it in turns to think of a problem you have on your mind at that moment. It could be personal (you cannot seem to get your daughter to bed on time) or work-based (you never seem to be able to get the attention of your boss). Start by describing the problem so that it is absolutely clear. For example, using one of the examples above, you might say: 'My daughter is always an hour late for bed and this is making me angry and her tired at school the next day; can you help me?'

Precise definition and your specific request for help are important elements here, so try to spend time in setting up the situation. Your friends or colleagues now take it in turns to offer you advice. Each time they do so, they use the formula, 'You might like to…' and you reply with, 'Thank you very much.' The use of 'you might like to' allows you to take a different view. It creates a sense of possibility, not compulsion. And saying thank you (even if you actually think it is a daft idea) prevents any critical evaluation of the ideas as they come in.

When you have heard ten or more ideas, stop the process and reciprocate by inviting someone else to try the exercise. This exercise almost always produces at least one helpful suggestion.

■ **New kinds of capital growth**

'Many think that stories are shaped by people. In fact, it's usually the other way around.'

Terry Pratchett

We now live in the age of knowledge management, where people, we are told, really are their firm's most important resource. Of course, organizations still need traditional sources of capital – money – to operate. But swilling around the organization is something at least as important: the knowledge that is going to generate next month's profits.

And bigger than knowledge management are the concepts of intellectual and social capital. For these kinds of capital encompass the future prosperity of organizations and nations. For them to grow, people need to be able to get the best out of the people with whom they live and work. Intellectual capital comes not just from the current swill, but also from the creative ideas which lie, as yet unrealized, in people's heads. As business writer Charles Leadbetter puts it: 'The engine of growth will be the process through which an economy creates, applies and extracts value from knowledge.'

Social capital involves all the networks, relationships and protocols that enable groups of people to live or work together successfully. Coined by American academic Robert Putnam in 1995, the central premise of social capital is that social networks have value. Social capital describes the collective value of all the people you know, 'the features of social life, the network, the norms and trust, that enable participants to act together to achieve shared objectives'.

Getting the best out of people has become an essential axiom of successful organizations rather than a nice-to-have one for model employers. For people can be creative, creative people have ideas and ideas are what lead to new products and services. And, in the domestic arena, families need to have the confidence to develop their own ideas on subjects as diverse as DIY, gardening, cookery, website design, fashion and music.

The zenith of feverish investment in ideas has probably been passed for now, with the bursting of the dotcom bubble of the 1990s. At the height of this trading fever, when venture capitalists were cheerfully investing several million dollars in half-worked-out web promises, it is rumoured firsttuesday.com was sold for $50 million. What was remarkable was that the First Tuesday initiative was little more than a simple idea about social capital – the bringing together of investors and those with business plans on the first Tuesday of the month – and the web technology needed to make it happen. The excessive early promise has evaporated and left us with a comparatively small number of really creative, sustainable ideas like amazon.com, lastminute.com, ebay.com and friendsreunited.co.uk.

Terry Pratchett suggests that people do not shape events as much as they would like to think. Yet, as all good storytellers know, narratives are about people, and this is especially so in the workplace where they can make or break a business. You need to be able to navigate your way more effectively through, around and with the people you deal with in your working lives (although, of course, we recognize that these kinds of skills largely apply at home, too) so that you can be more creative.

This does not mean that you have to exploit people. In fact, the opposite is true. Our approach is to explore those ways in which, by understanding more about the way your mind works and by adopting deeper, smarter and softer ways of communicating and motivating those around you, you can allow your creative self to develop and shine through (and get what you want, even if you do not always know what this is).

The living organization

We believe that organizations, as management guru Arie de Geus suggests in his book *The Living Company*, are not machines. Rather they are living entities, with their own sense of identity, their own capacity to act autonomously and a powerful ability to adapt, regenerate and survive. Living organizations value learning and creativity. And this tenet will thread its way through all we have to say.

Unless you are determinedly curmudgeonly, you will want to get the best out of people. In the eighteenth century, British economist Adam Smith defined wealth in terms of productivity (what you can produce). Today, more than two hundred years later, we are beginning to define wealth in terms of creativity and learning (the ideas you have and your knowledge).

The financial balance sheet has served us well enough in describing businesses concerned with production. But these are increasingly few in number. Many now provide services or sell their know-how as well. And some – the creative industries, for example – exist solely to trade in ideas. Nowadays we need a new kind of balance sheet that tells us about the intangible assets – the people – that go to make up an organization. How long do they stay? How motivated are they? Are they keeping up to date? How do they learn from projects that really stretch them? How good are the leaders and managers? Of course, we need to know some basic financial details, but increasingly this fails to differentiate between one organization and another. Interestingly, as we write, the British Chartered Institute of Personnel and Development has launched a major campaign to compel companies to report on their people management practices – their human capital.

One image currently in vogue with regard to the recruitment and retention of people is the idea that there is a 'war for talent'. This is both positive (it suggests that people really are important enough to go to war for) and extremely depressing (it implies that employers need to go outside their own organization to realize human potential rather than developing it within the organization).

As a creative person, you will want to grow and learn, developing your talent and realizing as many of your intelligences as possible.

■ Choose your peers wisely

'I choose my friends for their good looks, my acquaintances for their good characters, and my enemies for their intellects. A man cannot be too careful in the choice of his enemies.'

Oscar Wilde

At first sight you might appear to have little choice about who you work with. You are given a manager and you have to work in certain teams over which you have little control. But stop and think for a moment. Is this really the case? While you have to work with a few people, are there not many opportunities for choosing your colleagues? Creative people care about who they hang out with, although possibly not along the lines of Wilde's whims. (We read an interesting example of this truth recently. It described research into children's achievement levels at school. It turns out that the main indicator of their likely success is not their teacher or their class group but the peer group they chose to spend time in the lunch queues with.)

Who do you hang out with? We know that one of the most powerful methods of learning is through imitation. You see someone doing something clever and you copy it. You marvel at the way a colleague manages a difficult situation while still staying calm, and try to imitate it yourself. We also know that role models matter hugely. The kinds of behaviour that are encouraged by managers and other key people matter. They set the tone and will be widely copied. If you choose to spend time with those who are cynical about life and work, some of their negativity will inevitably rub off on you.

Which brings us to Pareto's law. You may have heard of this as the 80:20 principle – 80 per cent of results come from 20 per cent of our actions. Invented by Vilfredo Pareto, an Italian economist, after studying patterns of wealth in nineteenth-century England, this law reminds us that life is predictably unbalanced. Pareto found that 80 per cent of the wealth was controlled by 20 per cent of people. He then began to notice this pattern showing up in all sorts of other areas of life.

IBM was one of the first companies to exploit this principle creatively. In the early days of computing it discovered that 80 per cent of the time a computer spends processing is spent on 20 per cent of the operating software. Using this data they redesigned their systems to make sure that the parts that were likely to be most used were the fastest and most accessible. Think about your own computer today. As likely as not, you use 20 per cent of its functions for 80 per cent of your time! Good software developers know this and make sure that the most popular bits of programmes are the ones that are fastest and easiest to use.

The Pareto principle can be applied to people, too. Just stop and think about the teams you work in. Which 20 per cent do most of the work? Which 20 per cent are the most creative in your eyes? If you go through your working life assuming that the way people act is rational or that everyone you come into contact with is equally likely to be able to help you, you will be disappointed. Organizations, as we have seen, are living organisms that grow organically. They are predictable and unbalanced. You have a simple creative challenge: to decide which 20 per cent of people you choose to spend most of your time with.

■ Tuning in to creative trends

Author of *The Tipping Point*, Malcolm Gladwell suggests that we should think of people and their ideas as if they were an epidemic. As he says: 'Ideas and products and messages and behaviours spread just like viruses do.' Every epidemic has its tipping point, the moment when it shifts gear. One moment it is a few people with a cold, the next the whole workforce is suffering from it. And one of the principles of epidemics is that they only need a few individuals to be involved. So, for example, the first Harry Potter book was printed in very small numbers. A few children began to read it and thought it was really good. They told their friends, who in turn told theirs. And the rest is history.

In getting the best out of people it is helpful to know this. If you are trying to persuade people to do something and that something is to be discussed at a meeting, then it will be important to have talked it through with a significant minority of those who will be attending. Gladwell suggests that you should focus your energies on a particular kind of person, a maven. Mavens are the well-networked people who are constantly accumulating knowledge. They are always the first to know when there is an office affair or when someone is about to be fired. Mavens know where you can get the best deal for anything, because they are constantly talking and listening to their circle of contacts. (The Harry Potter example above showed that many children are very good mavens.) Creative people need to know who the mavens in their lives are, both at work and in their home lives.

NOW TRY THIS: A mental maven hunt

Relax for a moment. Close your eyes. Let the faces of all the people you work with swim before you. Imagine that you are listening to each one of them as they move past you.

Which of them are chattering away with news about this and that?

Who seems to have lots of contacts?

Think about who you go to talk to when you really want to find out what is going on in your organization.

Open your eyes. Did you find some mavens?

It all comes down to trust

'Trust is the bandwidth of communication.'

Karl-Erik Sveiby

Of course, trust is at the heart of all effective human relationships. Without it relationships simply cannot prosper. It is the bedrock on which all your dealings with people need to be based.

Households need trust to function effectively. Living organizations which trust their people get more out of them. Individuals who constantly show that they trust those around them and are trusted by their colleagues in return will have much better relationships. The great thing about it is that you can create a micro-environment of trust, so that, even in an organization where there is a culture of suspicion and disbelief, at the level of individual teams this need not be the case.

Trust is at the heart of the development of social capital. It is not just a nice, warm, cuddly feeling (important though this might be). There are a wide variety of quite specific benefits that flow from the reciprocity, information-exchange, ideas sharing and cooperation that are associated with trusting relationships.

Put most bluntly, where you find negativity, suspicion, lack of trust and low levels of team working, it is essential that you seek to transform this into more creative approaches of the kind we outline in this chapter.

E.M. Forster put it succinctly: 'One must be fond of people and trust them if one is not to make a mess of life.'

Making communication matter

'The major problem with communication is the illusion that it has happened.'

Albert Einstein

Many parents complain about the fall-off in communication between them and their children (especially when the children reach their teens), often citing busy lives, television and declining educational standards as the reasons. The impoverished interaction that takes place over hastily grabbed meals on the run was recently called 'the daily grunt'.

It can feel the same in the workplace. In the vast majority of organizations what passes for communication is laughably inadequate. Often it is little more than top-down briefings containing inadequate data and occurring well after events have happened. For communication to work it has to be genuine, two-way and timely. You need to know that your opinion will be, at the very least, listened to. And you need to have access to the richest possible stream of data available if you are going to be able to contribute most creatively.

Case Study

3M is well known for its history of innovation, from sandpaper to Post-It notes, scotch tape to sponges that use anti-microbial technology to stay clean. As you would expect, there are high levels of trust in the organization. William Coyne, senior vice president of research and development, emphasizes the need to create a rich climate of communication: 'Share discoveries with others in your group, as all may find different uses for them. 3M's philosophy is that the technologies belong to everyone in the corporation; 3M employees know that those who make contributions to advances across several business units tend to have more success in career advancement.' At 3M, employees are also empowered to make their own changes and encouraged to spend up to 15 per cent of their time, as they see fit, in activities that may generate new ideas.

Motorola similarly values good communication. To ensure that all managers listen to their teams, it has devised five key questions concerning their life at the company that form the basis of all one-to-one review meetings. These include: Do you have a substantial meaningful job? Are you respected as a person and employee? Is there training in place to make you successful?

These two organizations are, in different ways, playing a part in nurturing creativity.

A combination of good two-way communication and trusting respect for individuals is equally helpful in the home environment, too.

Effective one-to-one contact

For relationships to be truly creative there needs not only to be trust, but also clarity of purpose. To be an effective and creative communicator you need to be honest about your own needs, clear about the real underlying 'contract' between you and the person you are in contact with, and comfortable with the medium you are using.

The British Talent Foundation, a not-for-profit organization dedicated to helping people realize their potential, has a useful tool – Wants and Needs – for helping people to be clear about their wants and needs:

The tool works particularly well in relationships like those you find commonly between a person and their line manager. It allows you to say what you want ('I want to see if I can do this on my own') and what you need ('I need you to tell the rest of the team that I want to learn how to do this and not be undermined by others doing it for me'). At the same time, it encourages the person to whom you are talking to be open, too. ('I want you to show people what you are made of. I need you to tell me the minute things are getting tough.') Going through this process helps you to clarify your needs and helps to establish the underlying contract to the set of assumptions you are both working to.

NOW TRY THIS: What you want and need

Decide whether you would like to focus on your home or your work milieu. Then either think of someone you currently live with or picture a colleague. Try to choose a relationship that matters to you. If you choose someone from your workplace, your line manager might be a good idea.

Use the tool we have just discussed either to explore your needs and wants with them or, if you prefer, on your own, with you imagining what they might say.

Start with your own wants and needs and then move on to those of the other person's. Are there any big differences in your views?

What could you do about this?

Methods of communication

In today's world the prevailing media of communication are email and telephone. Yet we all know how important it is, in many situations, to be face to face with someone, especially when you are dealing with difficult or complex issues. As we invent more and more technological means of communicating with each other, the assumption made by many people is that the latest method must be the best. (Do you remember the invention of the answering machine – how people would often ring back to check that it really was you? Or in the early days of the fax, how they would want you to send a hard copy as well, as if the fax was not real?)

The most important and basic creative question you can ask people is this: 'What method of communication do you prefer?'

Asking someone how they like to be contacted also gives out other powerful signals of respect and consideration that will stand you in good stead – whatever it is you have to say.

The psychology of communication

Much of our communication, at home and in the workplace, involves asking other people to do things for us. We need help with a project, we want something typed up, we have to borrow something. Three simple rules underpin this basic activity. Each helps you to see how you can use your creativity so that it is more likely your colleagues will comply with your wishes.

Give before you ask

The first involves our instinctive behaviours. Why do so many magazines have a free gift attached to them? Why do people give you free samples? Why is it that when someone shows you an act of kindness you tend to remember it and want to help them out when the opportunity arises? Or when a waiter or waitress makes sure that you have a good table and brings you water that you have not asked for, you feel like tipping more at the end of the meal. Sociologists call this the reciprocation principle. You scratch my back and I'll scratch yours, as the old saying has it.

It is easy to see how this kind of socially bonding behaviour works well in close communities or among good friends and colleagues. Someone fetches you a coffee and you reciprocate. But think creatively about the people you work with that you do *not* particularly like. Would it work with them? Interestingly it seems that it does. Do a minor favour for someone or give a small free gift to someone and, even if they dislike or disapprove of you, it is much more likely that you will be able to persuade them to do what you want them to. So, remember, give before you ask, even if it is the last thing you'd like to do. Be creative. Try it out if you don't believe us.

Remember to say 'because'

The second rule is, at first, a surprising one. Ellen Langer and her colleagues carried out a simple experiment into the way we ask for favours more generally. Langer got people to see if they could jump the photocopying queue in a typical workplace. Researchers tried two different requests. 'Excuse me, I have five pages, may I use the photocopier?' (This was 60 per cent successful.) 'Excuse me, I have five pages, may I use the photocopier because I am in a rush?' (This was 94 per cent successful.)

Initially it seemed that the reason for the more effective queue-jumping was the 'because I am in a rush'. But Langer tried a third type of request, which points to an even more startling conclusion: 'Excuse me, I have five pages, may I use the photocopier because I have to make some copies.' Researchers using this sentence were also 93 per cent successful. The repetition of information already given made it clear that the vital word was, in fact, 'because'. Somehow this vague introduction of a reason is enough to produce an instinctively positive response in us. So, in your life and work, remember to say 'because'.

Tell bad news first

The third key idea underpinning communication is the contrast principle. Try this example. Imagine you have three buckets of water. One is cold, one lukewarm and the third is hot. Imagine you are putting one hand in the hot water and the other in the cold. Leave them for a few minutes. Now put both hands in the lukewarm one. (This might be your cue to go and try this activity for real.)

What happens next is that the hand that has been in the cold water thinks it is in hot water, and vice versa. In short, a slight contrast becomes a big difference when we encounter experiences one after the other. In terms of communication, there is something very important to learn here. It is this: if you have bad news, tell it first. Shop assistants know that the contrast principle sells goods. Have you ever bought a suit or an expensive item of clothing and then been asked whether you would like that tie or that brooch to go with it, and found yourself saying yes? They know that if they can sell us an expensive item first, then the second cheaper (but possibly still not that cheap) item will seem more reasonable. Some car sales people deliberately show customers cars they will not like so that the next one they see will seem better than it really is by comparison.

The contrast principle also works for communication. Ask for the most difficult or most expensive thing first and your subsequent requests or comments will seem much easier to respond positively to. Most organizations operate on the reverse of this principle, keeping the most difficult data to an inner circle. Meanwhile, the minds of all of their employees have been racing, inventing scenarios and explanations that are far worse than the real thing. The result is an unnecessary erosion of trust and lowering of morale.

NOW TRY THIS: Create a letter to your manager

Imagine that you have to tell your line manager something difficult. Let's call him John. A 'Dear John' letter might go something like this.

Dear John

I am sorry we have not managed to catch up with each other for the last few weeks, but things have been very bad for me.

I had to fire my whole team for gross professional misconduct after that dreadful incident with the suppliers that you may have heard about.

Then my son was expelled from his school and my husband left me for a younger woman.

And finally, as if that were not enough, it seems as if one of our contractors has been deliberately sharing sensitive commercial information with our competitors.

Actually, John, this is not quite true. My team is fine. My family are doing really well and our contractors are all working their butts off for us, extremely effectively, at the moment. What I really wanted to say was that I think I am going to be about 5 per cent down on my third-quarter financial targets and I wanted you to be able to put this disappointing situation in perspective.

Yours
Liz

Could you write a letter like this to your boss? Maybe, maybe not. But you could try to explore the thought processes underpinning it and, in so doing, use the contrast principle. Let your imagination run wild with this exercise.

Think of a situation when you have done something at work that has got you into trouble or not lived up to the expectations of your boss. Now exaggerate it so that it becomes ten times more serious.

Use this line of thought to write a 'Dear John' letter of your own.

Sometimes, of course, the act of writing a letter, even if you have no intention of sending it, can be a great creative way of letting off steam.

Develop soft talking to enhance creativity

How you communicate with people is critically important. For there is a growing recognition of the value of collective talk that is slower and more reflective. Where brainstorming and the like invite people to mentally rush around, producing ideas that are mostly hare-brained, a more tortoise-like conversation can deliver better ideas. 'More haste, less speed' is a maxim that applies here. Talking, listening and thinking at a more leisurely pace is characteristic of many traditional, tribal societies, and we are beginning to realize that not everything can be speeded up and still retain its quality. A Native American chief, Luther Standing Bear, summed up this very different mood of conversation thus:

'Conversation was never begun at once nor in a hurried manner. No one was quick with a question, no matter how important, and no one was pressed for an answer. A pause giving time for thought was the truly courteous way of beginning and conducting a conversation. Silence was meaningful with the Lakota, and his granting a space of silence to the speech maker, and his own moment of silence before talking, was done in the practice of true politeness and regard for the rule that "thought comes before speech".'

In his ground-breaking book *Creativity*, Mihaly Csikszentmihalyi interviewed a group of more than ninety exceptional individuals, and from this empirical research determined that one of the characteristics shared by the most creative people is their level of energy. Not surprisingly, creative people tend to have a lot of it. But importantly, he found that this energy is under their control. They are not always rushing around creating, but often prefer to seek quiet in their lives. 'They often take rest and sleep a lot... they consider the rhythm of activity followed by idleness or reflection very important for the success of their work.' Mixing sound and silence – the sociable and the solitary – provides most people with the kind of rhythm of talking, listening, thinking and reflecting that is conducive to their creativity.

Some people find that the act of quiet contemplation or prayer is the one that is most useful for them in harnessing their innermost creative self. Studies of meditators show that they can both see more clearly – their eyes are less clouded by hopes, fears and projections – and access playful imagery and metaphor more readily.

■ Thinking together: The value of dialogue

'It is proposed that a form of free dialogue may well be one of the most effective ways of investigating the crisis which faces society, and indeed the whole of human nature and consciousness today. Moreover, it may turn out that such a form of free exchange of ideas and information is of fundamental relevance for transforming culture and freeing it of destructive misinformation, so that creativity can be liberated.'

David Bohm

Creative organizations are increasingly using something called dialogue as the kind of communication that is most likely to get the best out of their people. At one level, dialogue is just a grand word for a good conversation. It traces its roots to ancient Greece and the perambulating discussions of Socrates and Plato, and yet can also be seen in today's reality television shows like *Big Brother*, where the audience members communicate directly with the programme makers to influence which one of the participants goes or stays. It is close to the kind of communication that is encouraged by internet networking sites such as MySpace and Facebook. It is the kind of approach that has led, in the past few decades, to breakthroughs in thinking in Northern Ireland and South Africa (where Nelson Mandela was one of its most skilful proponents).

David Miliband, MP, went on record as British education minister bemoaning that: 'One of the problems with our intellectual culture is that there is too much writing. There is lots of writing, but not enough talking, not enough discussion of ideas.' But, sadly, this phenomenon is not confined to the intellectual world. It is evident in our homes where the family supper is rapidly becoming a thing of the past. And it is clear to see at work, where people are often working so hard that conversation is staccato and impatient.

Dialogue is more than conversation, argument or discussion. In the sense we are using it, dialogue is a fairly recent term in organizational vocabulary. Business guru Peter Senge has called it 'genuine thinking together'. Physicist David Bohm argues that there are three essential ingredients to it:

- First, it involves everyone suspending their assumptions.
- Second, everyone treats each other as equals.
- Third, there is a role for a facilitator to keep reminding participants of the context and to help shape the flow of thinking.

At the heart of dialogue is the assumption that people have valuable ideas, and that the more an individual is engaged in an issue, the more they will become committed to getting the best solution.

The mood of dialogue

Dialogue is more a mood or a quality of conversation than a specific technique, though there are ways in which this mood – which is very different from the more normal feel of a discussion – can be encouraged. Everyone is familiar with the mood of dialogue. You feel it in a heart-to-heart conversation with an old friend. You occasionally catch it in a meeting in which suddenly everyone is sitting forward in their seats, totally engaged and bound together in a spirit of communal enquiry. Everyone is aligned: listening, learning, contributing, and willing to look with fresh eyes and to hold up their own taken-for-granted beliefs and opinions to challenge. People are living on the edge of their understanding, genuinely willing to be perplexed, to admit confusion, to dare to look underneath their reassuring 'position' to the greater complexity these positions are often designed to conceal and contain. This magical shift can happen easily in intimate situations; much more rarely does it occur in a student seminar or a business meeting.

Dialogue is basically a set of ground rules that encourages this mood shift to occur. The pressure to answer a specific question or problem is allowed to recede into the background. There may be a question to kick off the conversation, but then the focus is on the process of collective enquiry. Your job is to go with the flow of the conversation, listening to what has been said; resonating with it, so that you take time both to get a real feeling for where the speaker is coming from and to feel what their speech touches in you; noticing what reflex reactions you are inclined to make; questioning them, and finally offering the tentative fruits of this resonance back to the group. Differences of opinion or experience do not have to be either resolved or swept under the carpet: they are embraced as constituents of the greater complexity that people are trying to let themselves feel.

Often a facilitator is needed, at least to begin with, to model the process and to draw people's attention to the many habits of conversation – agreeing, disagreeing, correcting, free associating, commiserating, hectoring, storytelling and so on – which tend to get in the way of genuine dialogue. Gradually the members of the group allow themselves to become genuinely puzzled and engaged, to reveal their uncertainties, to hear the resonance with other people's uncertainties, and to join a journey of exploration that is both meaningful and collaborative.

Dialogue relaxes the boundary between hard and soft thinking, and by inducing a kind of collective reverie, allows softer thinking to become a communal, as well as an individual, experience. Out of this, better ideas –

ones that take account of more complexity and embrace differing needs and perspectives – can emerge.

Dialogue is becoming increasingly common in business meetings, especially where people are endeavouring to stand back from the need to respond to immediate problems and crises and think more strategically. To do so inevitably involves questioning more assumptions, and embracing more complexity and uncertainty, than busy people normally have the time (and perhaps the inclination) to do. Despite that, people sometimes find the process of dialogue strange at first. Once they have got the hang of it, and can feel the mood shifting, they can derive enormous benefit in terms of the quality of relationships as well as of ideas.

NOW TRY THIS: Comparing discussion and dialogue

Now that we have begun to explore some different kinds of conversation, see if you can become more sensitive to the shifting moods or tones which different types engender.

When you are taking part in group interactions, notice how people's body language signals their different kinds and degrees of engagement. Observe how their posture, their eye contact and their voice quality changes.

- Notice when there are pauses or gaps in the conversation: can you feel when people are really thinking and enquiring, rather than just arguing or contributing from fixed positions?
- See if you can turn this awareness on yourself. What is it that grips you or makes you genuinely *wonder* about things? How does it feel inside when you are in this state?
- Can you control the amount of time when you are in this reflective frame of mind, or does it just happen?

When you have the opportunity, involve people in a contrasting style of discussion. Find a practical problem at home, at work or with friends, and invite people to spray out as many suggestions as they can think of without evaluating either their own or other people's ideas.

- How does that feel? Is it successful?
- On a different occasion, see how it works if you deliberately slow down the pace of the discussion and make people listen to each other better. One 'rule' you might try is this: no one can contribute their own point of view until they have re-stated the last person's contribution to that person's satisfaction.
- What happens to the creative quality of the discussion if you do that?

Conclusion

Faced with a difficult or complex issue, your ability to manage the third dimension of your state of mind – your *sociability* – is very important. Who you choose to spend time with matters. Having a buddy will help you. Recognizing that you can influence the people you work and live with is vital. And learning softer, less adversarial modes of communication, such as dialogue, will be invaluable.

Flexible thoughts and an open mind are vital for success at work

Chapter 6
Creating ideas in practice

- Growing good ideas
- Using brainstorming and synectics
- The value of an open mind
- Take a break and slow things down
- How to think in threes or fours
- Use incubation time to unlock your brain
- Looking for outrageous opposites
- Action learning
- How to use double-loop thinking

'New ideas come into this world somewhat like falling meteors, with a flash and an explosion, and perhaps somebody's castle roof perforated.'

Henry Thoreau

In the last chapter we began to explore the situation in which you find yourself – your general social milieu – at home, with friends, with colleagues at work, and how you can choose to exercise the third of our three rhythms: the ability to move between the sociable and the solitary.

In this chapter we will be focusing exclusively on the pressures and opportunities of the contemporary workplace for your creative development and on a few techniques it may be helpful to acquire. You might think that every employer would be keen to support the development of their employees' creativity. Indeed almost all employers would say that they are *for* creativity. But the actual practice of much office life, when under pressure or when 'unobserved', is often fundamentally hostile to creative people. It is the softer approaches we have been advocating throughout the book that may be most conducive to the successful generation of ideas. The 'firm', as you might say, needs to become the 'soft' if it is to thrive today.

■ Creativity under threat?

If you were a Martian on a fact-finding tour, visiting a contemporary workplace whether in the USA, Europe, Australia or the Far East, you could be forgiven for thinking that human beings have indeed become very creative and have worked out how to generate and communicate ideas very well. For in your report you might comment favourably on three things.

The first is the way that, in many meeting rooms, you saw groups of workers creating wonderful new ideas by a process the earthlings called brainstorming. (Being a diligent Martian you will also record, in a separate note, that this was invented by Alex Osborn in the 1950s as a tool for developing ideas in the advertising industry.)

The second technique that will have caught your all-seeing central eye is a method of communication called 'powerpointing'. Invented by Microsoft,

Powerpoint is a brilliant way of reducing complex subjects to a heading and four main points (sometimes referred to as bullets) and offering opportunities for pictures and diagrams.

And the third is a phenomenon that has arisen as a result of the fact that earthlings have at long last invented mobile telephones. Sometimes, you will write, in the middle of their creative brainstorming sessions or even in their more private meetings, these phones ring, interrupting all activity around them to feed in the latest creative ideas from some kind of earthling talking database.

Ah, if only you had been able to send the intergalactically renowned University of Mars research team! For they, with their advanced forensic skills, would have discovered that brainstorming could be a hugely formulaic, ineffective and unsatisfying process, and would have observed how Powerpoint, far from being the creative communication tool you had thought it to be, can induce a kind of passive torpor among those it is projected at in which virtually nothing of meaning penetrated the minds of the earthling recipients. And, as for the phones, it is hardly necessary to recount their corrosively intrusive impact on the flow of conversation, dialogue or any other intimate kind of ideas exchange.

▪ Brainstorming to best effect

'Creativity is the marvellous capacity to grasp mutually distinct realities and draw a spark from their juxtaposition.'

Max Ernst

Of course, the idea of freeing up the muse by withholding critical judgement for a while is sound enough. But brainstorming, at least as it is often practised, has turned out to be less effective than had been hoped. Ideas are often produced in a manic whirl – the name 'brain*storming*' gives it this feeling – that is far too frenetic for the delicate process of resonance to get to work.

Brainstorming groups are likely to fall into a collective state of mind that is less, not more, conducive to the production of good ideas. Indeed, one of the main criticisms of brainstorming is that too many of the ideas it produces are dull or worthless. People simply stop thinking, in either hard or soft fashion. In the atmosphere of impatience the process induces, people are likely to give up too quickly. They throw out a few thoughts – preferably as bizarre as possible – and then sit back. But there is evidence that, just as with certain kinds of distillation, the first 'fraction' that boils off is not the most valuable. You have to let these quick ideas come and go before, in a more sustained and reflective mood, other possibilities that are more genuinely creative *and* relevant begin to bubble up.

Indeed, in the clamour of a brainstorming session it is all to easy for some people – perhaps the very ones who are most adept at using reverie to think softly and slowly – to take a back seat and contribute little or nothing. Those who contribute most might be relying on a kind of superficial verbal fluency, coupled, perhaps, with a need to occupy the limelight. And often these strong voices would induce a kind of 'groupthink', which forecloses on creative exploration rather than opening it up.

You also know how about half the population is unlikely to want to do its thinking out loud because it prefers to undertake it in the quiet of its own mind. And, for both of us, an enduring memory is of crumpled flipcharts that you just knew were never going to be used again, let alone be typed up, synthesized and circulated. There are variations of this technique which enhance its effectiveness.

Introducing synectics

Brainstorming's smarter and more complex sister is *synectics*. This is a kind of brainstorming that draws on analogies and metaphors to help trigger associations and imaginative relationships between apparently unrelated concepts and objects. The essential difference from brainstorming is that synectics encourages the focused use of criticism where brainstorming forbids it. Depending on how well it is facilitated, synectics can be an effective, if challenging, method of generating ideas. Typically questions and statements like these will be posed in order to seek out new connections:

What rules can you break? What would this look like in the abstract? What would happen if you made it bigger? What would happen if you moved the subject into a new situation? Or out of its historical, social, geographical setting? Sympathize with subject. Put yourself in its shoes. What would it be like if the subject had human qualities?

Both brainstorming and synectics can work. The trick is to know when to start and when to stop using them.

▦ Braindraining environments

In the last ten years there has been more emphasis than ever before on the need for ideas generation in the workplace. A simple search on the web throws up hundreds of organizations specializing in helping for-profit and not-for-profit organizations to become more creative. The challenge for leaders in the twenty-first century, as management guru Warren Bennis puts it, 'will be how to harness the brainpower of their organizations'. The 1990s was even designated the decade of the brain by President George Bush senior and the United States Library of Congress.

But at the same time as there has been heightened interest in the space between our ears, a number of powerful trends in the labour market have created a workplace environment which is arguably less, not more, conducive to creative brain activity than it was before. Layoffs after the bursting of the dotcom bubble, reductions in workforces occasioned by technology and globalization, massive changes in organizational processes, a public service 'modernization' agenda – all have contributed to uncertainty and high levels of stress.

The habit maps of organizations, like those of individuals, are not always as attractive when they are under stress as when they are more relaxed. Organizations which on the surface espouse values of openness, empowerment and distributed leadership, suddenly become old-style hierarchies.

On one level, this is nothing new. Back in the 1950s, Herbert Simon coined the term 'satisficing' to describe the general sense that, in the workplace, it is all right just to get by and put up with what will do rather than what is exciting or innovative. In these kinds of situations, there is pressure to go for a quick fix rather than a really good idea that goes to the heart of a tough issue.

But the default settings in many organizations are revealed in all their full horror when the going gets tough. They involve fear. They use command and control methods. They are not respectful of individual potential or creativity. They are very adrenaline-fuelled places where, unless individuals are wholly confident in the kinds of techniques we have been discussing in the first part of this book, they are unlikely to find much joy in a brainstorming session! Yet it is often in these environments that ideas have to be generated. Fear of failure is common. A lack of security and esteem is to be expected. And if decisions are regularly taken 'by someone higher up', there is a chronic lack of challenge, which is hardly conducive to the generation of ideas.

Abraham Maslow is generally credited as the first to have pointed out that creativity arises out of a basic human need to realize our potential (or, to use his term, self-actualize). As he puts it: 'This ability to express ideas and impulses without strangulation and without fear of ridicule from others turned out to be an essential aspect of self-actualizing creativeness.' Humanistic psychologists have gone further and suggested that, as we grow older, we potentially become less creative. Author and thinker Carl Rogers writes: 'This tendency may become deeply buried under layer after layer of encrusted psychological defences.'

It seems that, for ourselves and for the organizations we work for, satisficing is, all too often, the name of the game. So, as you seek to release your creative self, this will not satisfice!

■ Creative horizons

Received wisdom has it that an idea is a new thought, a result of intellectual activity, something that may lead to a Nobel Prize or a new patent. In truth, this is a very limited definition. In much contemporary writing about innovation, an idea is almost synonymous with a new product and something that will make its creator(s) lots of money.

This is not how we see it, especially in the workplace. While riches may well flow from creativity in some cases, so, too, may greater happiness or personal insight. An idea adds to the sum of human understanding. It is more than the sum of all that has been put into its creation. According to Arthur Koestler, the colossus of creativity thinking, creative ideas fall into three different domains. The first is artistic, the second scientific and the third comic. Koestler calls these the 'ah', 'aha' and 'haha' moments, stressing both the way in which idea generation crosses many boundaries and also the fact that humour is often involved!

When you are generating ideas, all kinds of complex things are going on inside your mind, especially in the area of the brain referred to as the cortex (the outer wrinkly bit around the edge). We have already begun to see how complex these kinds of process are. Many different parts of the brain are involved, depending on a number factors, including the language you are using, the degree of emotional involvement you have and your state of arousal.

Two important processes are at work. The first is the endless quest for novelty that each neuron in the brain is engaged in, expressed in terms of one neuron seeking to connect with another as sensory data are processed. The second is the brain's tendency to form patterns and, in the case of an idea, novel associations. It used to be thought that all of this was an activity of the right-hand side of the brain; we now know that it is much more complex than this. And we have seen how it is possible to encourage exploration of our inner-net of thoughts and feelings and memories as well as our store of conscious experiences.

▨ When hard thinking doesn't work

'There is no such thing as a logical method of having new ideas… Every discovery contains an irrational element or a creative intuition.'

Sir Karl Popper

One of the arts of being in touch with your more creative self is to know when to give up hard thinking. Give up too soon, and you won't have reached the impasse. You won't have created and magnetized the best possible problem representation, and you are (a) less likely to gain access to your inner-net, (b) less likely to set up the kind of fruitful resonance that throws up interesting associations and images, and (c) less likely to recognize a good idea or a solution for what it is, even if it does come your way. But persist too long with hard thinking and you won't be allowing yourself to tap the deeper wellspring of your creativity. The trouble is: there is no rulebook that tells you when the optimal point for switching modes has been reached. There are some signals, however.

Getting stuck

First, notice if you have got to the stage where you seem to be going round in circles (both individually and collectively). Is there a sense of being trapped within a view of the problem? Alan Watts once defined worry as 'the state in which thought whirls wildly around without issue'. If you are worrying in this sense, it may well be time to switch modes. Your thoughts may have a stale or over-familiar quality: you aren't coming up with anything new.

Many people are familiar with this in the context of the 'tip of the tongue' state, where you are trying to remember a name or a word and the wrong one keeps popping up instead. Then you realize that the smart strategy is to stop thinking about it head-on, and wait for the answer to pop magically into your mind at some later point. The tip-of-the-tongue phenomenon is a small symbol of the whole domain of creative problem-solving that we are talking about here.

(If you are a crossword puzzler, have you noticed how often a solution pops into your head, but it takes you quite a lot of hard work to 'figure out' *why* it is the right answer?)

Getting tired

The second pointer is whether you are getting tired, or beginning to lose concentration after a spell of analysis and scrutiny. The brain may be telling you that it is now smart to give up and have a rest – and smart people are well advised to heed the signals their brain is sending. Andrew Grove, the CEO who built Intel into the microchip goliath, says: 'My day always ends when I am tired, not when I am done.' A good manager's work is never 'done'; but work done in a state of increasing exhaustion becomes inefficient and uncreative.

■ What science says about hard thinking

Neuroscientists are willing to hazard an educated guess as to why hard thinking is effortful and draining. It is expensive in terms of the brain's resources. There are two kinds of activity that neurons and neuron groups can send each other: excitatory and inhibitory. Excitatory connections tend to 'turn on' surrounding concepts in the habit map. Inhibitory connections tend to suppress them. The brain's natural tendency is for activity in an epicentre to ripple outwards in an excitatory way, turning on other concepts as it goes. But obviously this has to be balanced by a tendency to turn active concepts off again – otherwise we would rapidly end up with all the lights in the house on at once, and lose any sense of direction, sequence or order to our thoughts. And we can also control the *width* of the spread of any pattern of ripples. If we use the minimum of inhibition, we get wide, shallow ripples. If we use much more so-called 'lateral inhibition', the neighbours and potential competitors of an epicentre are strongly muzzled, and we get more *focused*, more *sequential* and also more *conventional* trains of thought: hard thinking, in other words.

In hard mode, the activity of the brain is restricted to the habit map, and the brain as a whole functions like 'Venice', as a well-defined system of canals. The walls of the canals are not permanently cut into the surface of the brain, but have to be created on each occasion by building temporary stockades of inhibition around each active centre. And this is expensive in brain terms. It uses up more neurotransmitters, more of the brain's molecular energy stores, and requires increased cerebral blood flow. When people who have been studying hard complain of 'brain strain', they may well be speaking the literal truth. A feeling of tiredness or strain may be the brain's way of telling you that the batteries are running low and will soon need to be recharged.

This expensive 'trick' of sustaining a tight-focus frame of mind for a period of time is probably one that evolution has only learnt rather recently. Animals go into focused mode sporadically and for limited periods: when they are startled by an unfamiliar noise, or when hunting, for example. But their default mode is diffuse. They don't stay highly focused and intently alert for longer than they need. And when the need is passed, mature animals can relax and space out for longer periods without apparently getting bored.

Diffuse awareness is preferable as the default mode because it is mentally less expensive, and because it is more receptive to the unexpected. A cat, resting on the verge of sleep, is still exquisitely sensitive to small, strange noises, as well as, of course, the sound of its bowl being washed. Human beings have become much more adept than other animals at creating and maintaining a state of restricted awareness, and this may be one of the functions of the part of the human brain that distinguishes it most clearly from the brain of other species: the dramatically enlarged areas known as the frontal and pre-frontal cortex. These areas are known to be involved in focused activity, and in regulating the electrical activity of other parts of the brain. But it may be that many of us have allowed this specialized facility to become the default mode. We may have got it the wrong way round. We live in a state of chronically constricted awareness, and thus have become more tired, less perceptive and less creative than we need to be.

Becoming impatient

The third and final sign that it may be time to quit hard thinking is if you find yourself becoming impatient with the problem as it is, and trying to replace it with a neater, more familiar one that you do know how to deal with. If you succumb to the temptation to *force* the problem to fit the diagnosis, you may generate a solution of sorts, but when you implement it, the cracks will soon start to appear. In the business world, the fashion for 'heroic management', which imposes radical reorganization based on a quick appraisal of the situation or the pronouncements of the latest guru, is frequently of this sort. By the time the magic solution begins to fall apart, the culprit is two jobs down the track, with an enhanced reputation for 'tough', 'insightful' management skills. Sticking with the problem at the point of impasse, and allowing time to think softly, is less dramatic, but more intelligent.

Enough of what is not helpful in the workplace. Let's begin to look at what *is* effective in helping you to be more creative at work.

■ It's vital to keep an open mind

John Grant, co-founder of the award-winning advertising agency St Lukes, is clear that one of the most important preparatory stages in seeking to develop new ideas or insights is to expose yourself to as many different opinions or theories as possible: 'At the start of any project, the best approach is to become a sponge.' You never know where you are going to gain inspiration from. But it is likely that you will need to take something you have learnt from one domain and consciously or unconsciously transfer it to another. So, going to the theatre becomes a stimulus for a biochemist, reading a nineteenth-century novel stimulates thoughts about a new branding campaign, understanding the history of money gives insights for website development or visiting a gallery gives inspiration for an engineering challenge. Anita Roddick, founder of the Body Shop chain of ecological stores, is convinced of the commercial advantage in this kind of approach. She puts it bluntly: 'Go where your competitors can't or won't.'

Creative people know that drinking it all in is all-important. They enjoy just walking around, listening and watching. They are happy to stop consciously fretting about a particular issue and become the sponge that Grant describes. They recognize that it may be smarter to go home and relax than to carry on fretting at work. They know that it may only be after they have 'slept on it' that they will know what is in their mind.

Sometimes contemplating something apparently unrelated helps. Try this.

NOW TRY THIS: **Practising contemplation**

Think of one of the issues that is currently on your mind. It could be taken from your home or work life. Make a note of it and then put it out of your mind.

Now, look at one of the pictures in a newspaper's colour section for ten minutes without thinking about it. If thoughts pop into your mind, acknowledge them and let them go. Try not to get caught up in long chains of thought. See how much of the time you can stay openly and attentively engaged with the picture, giving it time to reveal itself. You may be surprised by what happens! Go back to the problem you wrote down. In what ways has contemplating the picture stimulated your thinking?

Scientist Friedrich Kekulé is famous for discovering that the chain of carbon atoms in a chemical called benzene joins up to form a circular ring. In his memoirs, he describes how he was sitting in front of his fire idly contemplating both the chemical problem and the flames. Gradually the flames dissolved into atoms which twisted and turned before his eyes in a snake-like motion. Then the snake appeared to seize its own tail and the strange form whirled in front of the chemist's eyes. Kekulé had seen enough to have intuited the structure of benzene that he had been working on so hard for so long.

Resisting the quick fix

In the workplace the stimulus for generating ideas is often a specific problem or challenge. The great temptation is always to move straight into ideas generation. Something will not work and you need to fix it immediately. Just by accepting this premise, you are inevitably narrowing your scope for creativity. A much better tactic is to start by working out what you already know about the issue. Then you can move on to find out what others already know. From there it is but a hop, skip and jump to moving outside the box around the problem and thinking more laterally about other situations in which people have been faced with similar challenges. (Look back at the two-ropes problem on page 83. You already had all the knowledge you needed to solve this. You just needed to apply it.)

Increasingly the term 'knowledge management' or 'tacit knowledge' is being used to describe the gene pool of good ideas that is washing around most organizations, if only you knew how to access it. This kind of knowledge ecosystem is rich in the algae and spawn necessary for creating ideas from within. Chris Mellor, CEO of the Anglian Water Group, found that, in the early days of his tenure at the company, it was commonplace for engineers to reinvent the wheel on a weekly basis when they were out on the road fixing leaks. He created the Aqua Universitas as a corporate university with, among other things, a role in safeguarding the corporate memory of good ideas.

We would often be better advised to spend time 'surfacing' the tacit knowledge we already have rather than striving to create apparently new ideas.

■ Breaking free from your habit map

'The mind likes a strange idea as little as the body likes a strange protein and resists it with similar energy… if we watch ourselves honestly we shall often find that we have begun to argue against a new idea even before it has been completely stated.'

Wilfred Trotter

It was Stanford University psychologist Robert Zajonc who first discovered, in 1968, something very perplexing about habits. His findings help us to understand why they can so easily become ingrained in us. He called it the 'mere exposure effect'. Apparently, we are more positively disposed towards things the more often we are exposed to them.

Case Study

Zajonc set up an experiment in which subjects were given a list of pairs of antonyms (words which mean the opposite of each other), such as forward/backward, up/down, in/out. The subjects were then asked to make clear which of the words in each pair had the more positive meaning for them. Meanwhile, Zajonc worked out which of the words occurred more frequently in English. His results demonstrated an amazing correlation between the words his subjects preferred and those that naturally occurred more frequently. So, for example, they preferred forward to backward, and the word forward occurs 5.4 times more frequently than backward. So it seems that our preferences are strongly influenced by forces over which we have little control (as advertisers know only too well).

Remember your first day in a new job and how you gradually learnt to accept and even like the strange ways people behaved there? Or how you gradually warmed to people you did not at first like? Or how, after a while, you began to see positive things in individual colleagues which you had not at first noticed? Much goes on in our mind of which we have barely any conscious awareness.

Sometimes it will be helpful if you can develop habit-breakers. These can take many forms. You might want to 'unlearn' something. Imagine you are on a camping expedition and have left your wash bag at home. How many different ways are there for you to clean your teeth without having access to your familiar toothbrush and toothpaste? Or when you are feeling most sure in a planned course of action in a particular project, start asking yourself 'why' questions and don't stop until you have thought of at least 30. You could deliberately share a plan with someone before you put it into action and ask them for feedback on your thought processes.

Stopping from time to time to review your habits is essential if you are to retain your creative self-awareness.

One habit that has almost become ingrained in our consciousness is that our brains are divided into two equal halves, one of which is creative (the right hemisphere) while the other is logical (the left side). Although it is certainly true that our brains, as Roger Sperry first suggested in the 1960s, have two halves connected by something called the corpus callosum, we now know that this is a huge oversimplification. Like many theories that depend on an 'either/or', this theory has huge limitations. Some of our most entrenched habits can be reduced to binary opposites like this. ('I always sleep on the left-hand side of the bed', 'I prefer wine to beer', 'I like classical not contemporary dance').

Try this exercise to free up your mind from the power of two.

NOW TRY THIS: Thinking in threes or fours

Think of a real dilemma currently facing you at work, one where you are considering two possible courses of action.

Threes: Now close your eyes and think of all the other options you possibly can. Don't give up even if it is hard work.

Let's suppose you were wondering which of two possible methods to adopt for the marketing of a new product. You might start by reluctantly adding at least one other method. Then you could force yourself to add another and see what this does to your thinking. Settle on one of these extra ideas and add it to your original two. Open your eyes. Has this helped?

Fours: You are now going to see what happens to your thinking when you play with the idea of four. Think of another issue you are currently wrestling with where you have a stark choice between two opposites (for example whether to travel by train or car).

Now put a cross in the middle of a piece of paper. Think of a reason why you might prefer one method of travel to another, like, 'It's easier for me to work/relax on a train'. Then think of the opposite.

Use a diagram like the one below to play with the respective advantages and disadvantages of possible course of action. When you have done this once, change one pair of labels and try again.

Sellar and Yeatman's classic comic history of Britain, *1066 and all that*, uses the idea of paired opposites to great effect when, in recounting the English Civil War, it describes the Roundheads as right but repulsive and the Cavaliers as wrong but romantic. These four words can be illuminating when applied to two contrasting courses of action even today.

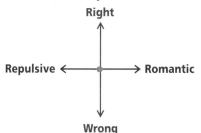

Another kind of habit that can get in the way of new thinking is the phenomenon of functional fixedness. You have already met this in the two-rope problem, but here is an even more effective demonstration of the effect.

NOW TRY THIS: Holding the candle

Look at the picture below. Using only the items shown, how can you fix the candle to a door so that it will not drip wax on to the floor?

Did you work it out? If not, the answer is on page 173. The small box which holds the tacks can also be used in other ways. This puzzle acts as a useful metaphor for the way our own daily thinking can proceed if we are not careful. Perhaps you could apply this in your own work. What would happen if you stopped thinking about the customer as the receiver of a service and started to see them as a partner, helping you to shape the service? Or, perhaps, you look again at the waiting room in your office and see it as a place for a short nap or a chance for patients to use the web, or as a library?

The more you can spot your own habits the better. And in the spirit of using soft approaches more often, don't worry if the answers do not come to you immediately. Sleep on it. Here's one more exercise for you.

NOW TRY THIS: Folding your arms the other way

Read this through first and then try it out from memory.

Sit on a chair with a straight back and with your legs parallel to the floor. Now cross your legs. Can you cross them the other way? (Of course you can.)

Now stand up with your hands by your sides. Relax for a moment, Then fold your arms. Unfold them. Fold them again. Do you have a favourite way of folding your arms? (Most people do.)

Now try folding them the other way. You may need to practise this for a while.

It is a little-known fact that most people go through life only ever learning how to fold their arms one way. This is because, as soon as we get tired, we drop our arms to our sides. The next time we want to fold our arms, we do so just like we have always done. A pattern has become a habit. Folding your arms the other way is another strong metaphor for the importance of breaking free from your habit map.

Spend a few moments thinking about the habits of those with whom you work most closely. How can you help groups of people in an organization to 'fold their arms the other way'? In other words, how can you get those you work with to try different ways of doing things?

And what about yourself? How do you go about solving problems? Try this exercise, suggested by Stanford academic James Adams, to help you reflect on the way you approach problem-solving. You might like to try it with a colleague over a coffee break.

NOW TRY THIS: Stepping out together

A man and a woman are standing side by side. They begin walking in the same direction. They both start off by putting their right foot on the ground. For each two steps of the man, the woman takes three steps.

How many steps does the man take before both of their left feet reach the ground at the same moment?

How did you go about solving this? Did you find a partner and pace it out? Draw pictures on a piece of paper? Plot it mathematically? Use your fingers to mimic the legs of the two people? Or some other ingenious method? Sometimes the smarter approach is to come at a problem from a number of different angles and not get set on any one particular method.

■ Keeping open-minded for as long as possible

'I am open-minded on all questions I care nothing about.'

Mason Cooley

As the celebrated aphorist reminds us, it is easy to be open-minded until you get closely involved in something. Yet you know that it is a smart thing to do to delay your gratification (remember the famous candy experiment we described on page 41). And, in Chapter 1, you found out that developing a habit of keeping your mind broad and open was a key part of becoming more creative. Now you need to put all this into practice at work.

It is a true, if unfair, fact that some of us find being open-minded easier than others. Think back to the brief explanation we gave you of the Myers–Briggs Type Indicator on page 125. Another of the contrasting pairs of traits is Judging and Perceiving. For it appears that we tend to favour different ways of making sense of the world. If your personality is instinctively to prefer 'judging', then you will like to plan in detail, take quick decisions, move to closure in a discussion quickly, be definite and stick to your schedules. If you are a 'perceiver' by nature, then you will prefer to wait and see, be flexible and adaptable, be open-ended and spontaneous, seeing all rules as there to be broken.

Both approaches are valid and, in different situations, one or other may be more appropriate. But there is a strong argument that, in today's fast-moving world, the approaches that go with perceiving may be especially important to learn if you want to be more creative at work. Certainly they will help you when you are trying to generate good ideas (and corporate culture, all too often, tends to be 'judging').

Sometimes it is a matter of common sense that, if you are too quick off the mark, you will get the wrong end of the stick, as this simple story illustrates.

Once upon a time four blind men came upon an elephant and tried to work out what it was. The first man, feeling a leg, was convinced that it was a tree. The second, grasping a tusk, thought it was a spear. A third, wrapping his arms round a wriggling trunk, warned his friends that it was a snake. And the fourth, touching the soft skin of the elephant's ear, pronounced it to be a fan.

If only they had taken their time, pooled their knowledge and got a fuller, more detailed picture of their mystery object!

Incubation

> 'Everyone was up to something, especially, of course, those who were up to nothing.'
>
> *Noel Coward*

Having good ideas takes time. Creative people often talk of the importance of 'incubation' or 'gestation', by which they mean the period during which no mental activity relevant to the problem seems to be going on, but into which erupts or sidles, 'out of the blue', something that feels distinctly relevant. Rita Levi-Montalcini, 1986 Nobel laureate in medicine, summed it up exactly when she said: 'You've been thinking about something without willing to for a long time… Then, all of a sudden, the problem opens to you in a flash, and you suddenly see the answer.'

There are actually four ways in which incubation – taking a break – helps in the process of generating ideas. First, you might be suffering from brain fatigue, and a break gives the brain a chance to recharge its batteries and return to the fray refreshed. Second, you might have got locked into a way of sensing or construing the problem that is preventing you from seeing the solution. The more you try, the more you are spinning your wheels, and the deeper you make the mental rut in which you are stuck. Taking a break gives this fixed viewpoint a chance to dissipate, and you can then come back to the problem with a more open mind. There are a number of studies which have now confirmed that, over periods of up to half an hour, incubation can definitely work in this way.

NOW TRY THIS: Practising incubation

Below are ten examples of what are called 'rebus problems'. Each revolves around a visual pun, which, unpacked, reveals a familiar phrase. For example, the rebus YOU JUST ME can be read as the phrase 'just between you and me'.

Give yourself 30 seconds to work on each problem. Hopefully, at the end of five minutes, there will be some that you have not been able to solve. Take a break for 15 minutes, during which time you are not to work consciously on the problems. Then come back and have another go. See how many you can get the second time round. Reflect on those you got after the break. What was it that stopped you solving them originally, and what shift had taken place in the second round that allowed you to see the solution? Was there an assumption or an approach that you were able to give up after the break? (See page 173 for solutions.)

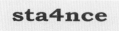

```
             1234567890
sta4nce      12safety90
             1234567890
```

When Steven Smith of Texas A&M University carried out this test as a properly controlled experiment, people were much more likely to solve the problems they failed on the first round after a break than if they came back to them immediately. And the longer the break, the better they did. The break was particularly successful for problems where Smith had originally provided people with a 'helpful hint' which was actually misleading.

The third way in which incubation works is much more random. A stray thought or a random occurrence connects with you. It is rumoured, for example, that James Watson and Francis Crick gained their insight into the helical structure of DNA while sliding down the banisters of a spiral staircase in Cambridge and daydreaming of the Nobel Prize. Sometimes you know what the crucial fragment of experience is, or, in retrospect, was. But often the key is so insignificant in itself, and the view through the door which it has unlocked so overwhelming, that there seems to have been no trigger at all. The mathematician Henri Poincaré told how the solution to a problem he had been working on very hard came to him when he was forced to give up work for a few days and take a trip. 'The changes of travel made me forget my mathematical work. Having reached Countances, we entered an omnibus to go some place or other. At the moment when I put my foot on the step the idea came to me, without anything in my former thoughts seeming to have paved the way for it.'

The trigger may go unnoticed especially in the fourth kind of incubation: where the key is furnished not by an external event but by a fleeting thought or image generated internally. The process is the same, but the mood is different. Often the crucial idea comes in a state of reverie, in which the problem is not completely forgotten, but provides a kind of background against which a rather uncontrolled play of ideas or images takes place.

Outrageous ways to gain perspective

'Keep on the look out for novel and interesting ideas that others have used successfully. Your idea has to be original only in its adaptation to the problem you are currently working on.'

Thomas Edison

Our survival as a species has been partly because we are very efficient in the way we use and discard our ideas. If they do not work, we cast them aside. If they seem to be far-fetched from our own experience we tend to reject them. Edward de Bono famously introduced the made-up word 'Po' for people to use when trying to generate ideas. Po gives its user permission to be outrageous. With hints of words like 'suppose', 'hypothesis' and 'possible' Po means 'I know that what I am about to say sounds ridiculous but let's see where it takes us'.

So, in an organizational context, you might say things like: Po, put the customer second, Po, be more expensive than our competitors, Po, make patients wait longer for treatment. Try this technique the next time you are in a meeting where it is clear that some creative thinking is required.

UK-based innovation company The Mind Gym deliberately uses this approach as part of an attempt to help people who describe themselves as logical thinkers to become more creative.

NOW TRY THIS: Outrageous opposites

Choose an issue from your workplace that you have already explored in this chapter. Make a list of some of the ideas you came up with to help you deal with this issue.

Now think of outrageous opposites to them. So, if your solution to whether to use the car or the train was to go by car, then an outrageous opposite might be to walk. Don't worry that your suggestions seem odd, funny or just plain daft.

When you have got a reasonable number of outrageous opposites, review them carefully. Do they contain the seeds of any interesting possible directions for further exploration?

Try them out on your colleagues. You may be surprised.

Some people find that creative connections come more readily if they are doing rather than thinking. Some people fiddle or doodle. Some people think best when they are just messing about with physical material or resources. Leonardo da Vinci would doodle for hours in ways that were apparently unconnected to his current projects. Recently, London's Victoria and Albert Museum gained creative inspiration by giving people digital cameras and just asking them to take pictures of whatever took their fancy on the streets. By rifling through these images, a great many creative ideas were generated.

▪ Action learning

Action learning has been around for a long time, but it remains one of the most powerful strategies for generating ideas and releasing your creativity. Action learning involves working on real problems, and is a form of learning by doing. Pioneered by UK academic Reg Revans, it is a process of collaborative enquiry in which it is assumed that the person bringing the problem to the group does not currently have the expertise necessary to solve it, or, if they do, that they need help to achieve this.

Typically, this is how it works. A small number of employees, often from different organizations, come together. The group establishes a trusting and confidential atmosphere in which it is safe to share difficult issues. Individuals take it in turn to describe one or more real business or organizational issue they are currently struggling with.

The group then decides which one (or more) of these they would like to tackle. In some cases the combined group expertise will be enough to provide useful answers to individual issues. But often it will only be able to go so far, because the problem being described is either wholly new or very specialized or so complex that a process of collaborative enquiry is called for.

Action learning is profoundly different from other forms of organizational learning or training. It is a move away from the dependence on available expertise and on hard approaches to thinking, towards the softer and more honest disclosure of doubts and sharing of uncertainty. It is based on the radical concept that L = P + Q, ie *Learning* requires *Programmed knowledge* (routine knowledge in use) and *Questioning insight*.

There are many books about this method which would give you more detailed support if you like the sound of it. There is even a University of Action

Learning at Boulder, Colorado if you want to find out about the method in greater depth.

One of the many benefits of action learning is the way it recombines doing and learning, because all too often problems remain either theoretical or practical.

■ Double-loop thinking

The soft creative strategies we have been discussing are all capable of standing on their own. However, there is a powerful tool that operates at a more strategic level than all of these – with the exception of action learning. This is the idea of 'double-loop thinking' as invented by Chris Argyris.

Double-loop thinking (as opposed to single-loop thinking) is all about thinking about what it is you are doing in a way that forces you to explore the underlying patterns of systems and situations. (If the photocopier breaks down, a single-loop response would be to fix it, while double-loop thinking would lead you to consider whether you should actually be printing rather than copying, if it would be cheaper to out-source it, whether you really need the copies and so on.)

Double-loop thinking involves reflection and challenge. In one loop we are doing the thinking and in the second loop we are observing ourselves doing the thinking. We are watching what we do, how we do it, how we feel as we do it, all while we are doing it.

Say you were thinking of changing the car you drive for work. Double-loop thinking would have you challenging your need to change it when a) you already have a reliable car, b) your current car is perfectly comfortable and c) there is good public transport in your area which would be much cheaper than running a car.

Or you might be faced with an issue like the need to save yet more costs – increasingly the norm in business today. The single-loop response will be probably be a) to sack some people, b) to put off all investment and c) to pretend that life can go on as normal. Recognize this? The double-loop solution could involve a) more, not less, investment, offset by new models of public–private working, or b) redeploying and retraining existing staff, or c) many other things which we have not even thought of.

Standing back from problems and getting to their underlying causes is often what is really required. It may well entail you in challenging the definition of the problem you have been faced with. For you may be presented with a symptom rather than the cause.

NOW TRY THIS: Double-looping

Close your eyes and relax.

Imagine you were working in a perfect organization. Everyone is fantastic and all the systems work wonderfully. (We realize that this may be a feat of the imagination!)

Now think of your actual place of work, or any other location of your own choosing. Make a list of the five things you would most like to 'fix' about its systems (a bit like you did when you thought up your own bug list on page 40).

What would the single-loop solutions be to each of the five? What would the double-loop version look like? Try this with a colleague or friend.

Ideas come to us in many shapes and sizes. Most employers want their employees to have good ideas. Some, we fear, are still threatened by the prospect of being challenged, but many employers at least pay lip-service to the idea of making an environment in which creativity can flourish. They may barely go beyond brainstorming. If you are looking for more enduring techniques, then dialogue, soft talking, incubation, action learning and double-loop thinking are powerful techniques you can use.

But the real answer to having good ideas at work lies inside you, in your ability to develop the creative habits we described in Chapter 1 and to use the *soft focus* and *inward orientation* approaches you have been learning throughout *The Creative Thinking Plan*.

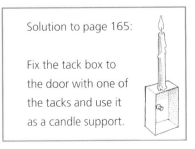

Solution to page 165:

Fix the tack box to the door with one of the tacks and use it as a candle support.

Solutions to pages 168-9:

For instance
Forgive and forget
Up for grabs
Safety in numbers

For creativity to flourish in your workplace, it must be conducive to developing new ideas

Chapter 7
Create an innovative work environment

- Is your workplace creatogenic or creatocidal?

- What makes work plus, minus, interesting?

- The art of past-tensing

- Be wary of too much order

- Use your voice

- The brain loves patterns

- Avoid cynicism

- Find your rhythms of pressure and ease

'Fear is the main source of superstition, and one of the main sources of cruelty. To conquer fear is the beginning of wisdom, in the pursuit of truth as in the endeavour after a worthy manner of life.'

Bertrand Russell

In this chapter, we focus on the *creative context* of your working environment, whether you have a 'conventional' job or whether you are one of the growing number of portfolio workers for whom your office is your home. We focus on three critical aspects of the creative environment: the use of space, the use of language and the management of time. For how creative we are depends on where we find ourselves, and as most people find themselves at work for many hours a week, it is important that you take all necessary steps to 'secure' this environment.

In the natural world, ecology is critically important. Provide certain wild-flower habitats and the bees will follow. Grow native trees and they are more resistant to disease and pests. Tamper with one element of the food chain and you upset the ecological balance. The plants you choose are critically important in creating a natural eco-system. In the workplace, the challenge must surely be to provide the kind of habitats most suited to creativity.

We believe that, just as some creatures thrive in certain habitats, so creative people will want to shape the workplace habitat in which they spend significant amounts of their time. The ecology of creativity is complex. Nevertheless there are positive environments – we call these *creatogenic* – and negative ones – we call these *creatocidal*. Sadly it is all too easy for organizations to include an element of fear, which inevitably causes much creativity to go underground.

▪ Features of creatocidal environments

As we have sometimes done in earlier chapters, let's start by looking at the opposite of what we want to explore, at what a creative workplace is not. Apart from the hugely important issue of trust, the glue that binds any community together and something we have already touched upon, here are four things which are the enemy of creativity at work and which conspire to create a creatocidal environment.

Constant distraction

The first, seemingly trivial, matter is the curse of constant distraction. A symptom of this is people who never give you their undivided attention because they are half watching their emails coming in and constantly picking up their phone. Distractions are inevitable, and, indeed, the creative thing is to plan for them. But if a state of being distracted becomes your way of being at work, it will be impossible to see things through or go with the flow of a train of thought.

Lack of cooperation

The second enemy is the almost institutional lack of cooperation that exists in many organizations. So much of what is important in an organization sits just below the surface of its informal structures in the tacit knowledge of its employees, who will inevitably come from different professional or administrative groups. It is tied up in the memories of the mavens who work with you. To access it requires cooperation. Some workplaces have become so tribal that a communication from one department triggers an allergic reaction from someone in another one. The result is lack of cooperation and low creative output. Yet as Thomas Jefferson reminds us: 'If nature has made any one thing less susceptible than all others of exclusive property, it is the action of the thinking power called an idea. No one possesses the less, because every other possess the whole of it. He who receives an idea from me, receives instruction himself without lessening mine; as he who lights his taper at mine, receives light without darkening me.'

The cartoonist Dilbert has long made fun of autocratic managers, and with some justification. You can doubtless picture the scene as just such a manager insists that you get on with your 'work' when you are actually in the middle of a really creative thought which, if only you were allowed the time to see it through, would save the company millions of dollars. In some organizations we know, a certain macho style has been allowed to go unchecked and, inevitably, leaves a trail of dysfunctional thinking behind it.

Good managers know that their support is crucial for the fostering of creative solutions. They become good at knowing how to nurture ideas and leave enough space around their team for creative approaches to blossom. As

George Prince, one of the founders of Synectics, summed it up: 'Seemingly acceptable actions such as close questioning of the offerer of an idea, good-natured kidding about someone's idea, or ignoring the idea – any action that results in the offerer of the idea feeling defensive – tend to reduce not only his speculation but that of others in the group... The victim of the win–lose or competitive posture is always speculation, and therefore idea production and problem-solving.' But securing the environment is not a task solely for managers. It is too important for that and depends on the creative energies of all who work in it.

High levels of stress

Thirdly, and not surprisingly in an age of stress, high levels of stress are counter-productive. Of course there will be times when, to fulfil a demanding project or complete a complicated order on time, you get stressed. But if this becomes endemic, then for employees it will begin to equate to a lack of control. And if employees feel disempowered they are hardly likely to want to share their creative ideas. As we have seen throughout the book, it is a question of balance and flexibility.

Environment of fear

The fourth and most corrosively negative feature of an environment is fear. Fear affects our productivity, our communication and our ability to create. It goes to the heart of our emotional well-being. Fear, at a basic physiological level, is the perception that there is an external threat to our well-being. It produces a predictable 'fight or flight' response and generates lots of the hormone adrenaline. You become more defensive, more aggressive and much less creative. You can see this in organizations where there is poor morale, resistance to new ideas, lots of negative gossip, a reluctance to admit to mistakes and a natural inclination to blame others. Conversations in such organizations happen only in the margins, rarely in formal meetings where managers dominate conversation with set-piece and often rather dull presentations.

■ Herzberg's 'motivators' and 'hygiene factors'

Psychologist Frederick Herzberg famously showed that satisfaction and dissatisfaction at work nearly always arose from different factors, and were not simply opposing reactions to the same factors, as had always previously been thought. He demonstrated that certain factors motivate – he called these 'motivators' – while others tend to lead to dissatisfaction – 'hygiene factors'. Hygiene factors would include things like getting a proper salary, having paid holidays or having access to a canteen. Motivators, on the other hand, include having a good relationship with a line manager, feeling valued in your work and having your personal development needs catered for. Herzberg's research proved that hygiene needs are a necessary minimum requirement, because employees are unhappy without them, but once these are satisfied the effect is short-lived and they are not necessarily happier, more creative or more productive.

A recent workspace satisfaction survey of six hundred managers, carried out by Stanhope and ICM for *Management Today*, had these results:

Feature	Really want	Actually get
Relaxation and thinking space	56%	20%
Gym	53%	14%
Restaurant	41%	31%
Child/elderly care	27%	6%
Shower	27%	39%
Cultural activity	12%	7%
Concierge services	9%	3%

These features of the corporate environment are clearly hygiene factors. They sit alongside salary, paid annual holidays and sick leave as the *sine qua non* of acceptable working. But they do not mean that the environment has been secured for creative working and is creatogenic. Far from it.

A food analogy demonstrates what we mean. Let's assume that you want to be as healthy as possible, so you will always want to eat food that is 'clean' and hygienic. But this in itself will not be sufficient to make you healthy. You might exist on a diet of 'clean' sugar and 'clean' meat. Yet the motivators to becoming truly healthy might be more like whether the meat you are eating is organic or not, or what the balance of your fruit and vegetable intake is, and so on.

To help to bring about the motivators to your creativity in the workplace, we need to look in more detail at the underlying issues. You might be surprised to see how many things you can do to secure your environment.

Features of creatogenic environments

For creativity to flourish, the environment must be conducive to ideas. While this is a statement of the obvious, it is an important one. It needs to feel more like a greenhouse – where tender shoots are nurtured and allowed to grow with extra support – than a hothouse – where exotic fruits are forced at times and in ways which do not seem natural.

Case Study

Computer giant Hewlett-Packard printed out these 'rules' in their 1999 annual report. Its workplace is described as a 'garage' in honour of the Palo Alto garage in which the company's founders, Bill Hewlett and Dave Packard, created their first product.

RULES OF THE GARAGE

Believe you can change the world.

Work quickly, keep the tools unlocked, work whenever.

Know when to work alone and when to work together.

Share – tools, ideas. Trust your colleagues.

No politics. No bureaucracy. (These are ridiculous in a garage.)

The customer defines a job well done.

Radical ideas are not bad ideas.

Invent different ways of working.

Make a contribution every day. If it doesn't contribute, it doesn't leave the garage.

Believe that together we can do anything.

Invent.

This is a decent attempt at creating the framework from which a creatogenic culture can emerge.

NOW TRY THIS: How ideas-friendly is your workplace?

Try this exercise with some of your colleagues at work.

Look at these examples of inventions that did not quite come up to scratch. They were possibly good answers to questions different from those they were originally designed to answer. Edward de Bono uses the example of the child who drew a 'silly' wheelbarrow with the wheel at the back, near the pusher, not at the front. While not ideal for some purposes, the revised barrow is actually rather good for carrying relatively light loads round tight corners (such as you might find on narrow walkways which make right-angled turns).

In 1970 Dr Spencer Sylver at 3M discovered a glue that didn't stick. He sent it round to other 3M labs but nobody could find a use for it. Ten years later another 3M employee, Arthur Fry, was continually irritated at the way his little strips of paper kept falling out of his choirbook, and losing the place. He had a vague memory of Sylver's silly glue... and the Post-It note was born.

The drug minoxidil was developed to lower blood pressure, but it had a powerful side effect that did not please everybody: it stimulated hair growth. Now it is in great demand by balding males.

What else could the 'silly' wheelbarrow be useful for? Come up with some of your own silly inventions. Or take some everyday inventions that seem to you to be rather unsuccessful. Have fun devising alternative uses for them. Then see what others in the group think they might be solutions to.

Did undertaking this kind of exercise feel okay within your working environment? If so, why? If not, why not?

Environments are personal

There have been a number of significant trends in workplace design in recent years. These include a move towards open-plan working, the abolition of private secretaries and the democratization of technology, with printers, fax machines and scanners liberally spread around offices. 'Hot-desking', or 'romping' as it is also being referred to, is a term that has only recently entered the language to describe the process of living out of a laptop computer and not allocating workers any personal office space at all. At the same time, some companies have begun to invest in more creative design approaches, ensuring that employees not only have access to the kind of benefits listed in the survey on page 179, but also sit and meet in attractive spaces while they are working.

Some organizations have experimented with meeting rooms with no chairs (to reduce the time spent on meetings) and informal meeting spaces with comfortable soft chairs, plants and espresso and water machines (so that employees will want to share their all-important informal findings).

For some people, hot-desking in an open-plan space is a pleasure, for others it is a creative nightmare. And the same is true for almost all aspects of our choice of space. It turns out that environment is a very personal matter. Famous figures from the past have, for example, had very different requirements for the perfect creative space. Dr Johnson needed a purring cat, Proust liked a cork-lined room and Schiller worked on a desk full of rotten apples. Kant sat up in bed with his blankets arranged just so. Writers Coleridge and Huxley needed drugs.

NOW TRY THIS: Creating your perfect working environment

Create a picture in your mind's eye of what your perfect working environment would be like. How would you like to feel in it? It might be a good idea to flip through the pages of glossy magazines for inspiration.

Use these questions as prompts to help you.

Do you like noise or quiet? Do you like privacy?

Do you need fresh air? Do you like access to the outside? Do you like a view? What kind of view do you like?

What about the style of furniture: modern, trendy, classic, functional, personal? Do you like plants and pictures?

Do you need different spaces for different activities? For different moods? Do you like to be able to get up and draw things out in a flip chart or on a wall space? Do you like moving around?

Do you mind which floor you are on? How much light do you like?

How close to your perfect space is your current working environment? What steps could you take to improve it?

Sadly there is no hard evidence that beautiful environments inspire creativity, although there is growing evidence from research into healthcare that they aid healing. Designer and researcher Roger Ulrich, for example, has shown that patients benefit from simply *looking* at gardens and plants. It seems only common sense to assume that there should be workplace benefits from an attractive environment too.

Empirical evidence suggests that different environments are either more or less conducive to different kinds of creative thinking. Take a moment to re-read pages 10–11 of the Introduction where we outline the three different dimensions of states of mind – *Focus*, *Orientation* and *Sociability* – before you begin this exercise. Also, hold on to the kind of images you were generating in the last exercise.

NOW TRY THIS: Matching the environment to your state of mind

Go through each of the different kinds of dimensions you have been exploring, if necessary recapturing the approach from one of the earlier chapters where the dimension was described. Think about the colours, shapes, sounds, smells that come to mind. Consider the role for other people in the environment and their impact on the kind of atmosphere that you would like to have. So, for example, a librarian, an office manager or a canteen manager would play obviously different roles and make similar environments feel different by dint of the way they influenced the space.

Focus
What kinds of space would seem most helpful to you when you are in soft focus mode, trying to become dreamy, playful and receptive to ideas? What about the reverse, when the quality of your mind is sharp, purposeful and absorbed in a single experience?

Orientation
Are there differences when your attention is focused inwards rather than outwards? What kinds of environment work best when you are busily absorbing information? And what about when you are more inward-looking and reflective, mulling things over and searching for deeper meaning and new connections?

Sociability

When your mood is solitary, what is the implication for the environment? How is this different from when you are more sociable, keen to kick ideas around and to immerse yourselves in other people's perspectives?

How are the environments different? Is there anything consistently different from being in soft, inward-looking, solitary mode from when you are hard, outward-looking and sociable?

Now think about what you can do to ensure that you create (or have access to) the kinds of environments that most suit the various states of mind that you will be wanting to have.

■ Getting away from it all

There has been a recent trend for businesses to take staff away to a nice country-house hotel for so-called 'away days' with colleagues to think 'creative thoughts' – sometimes called 'blue-sky' sessions – about the future of the organization. In our experience these kinds of events can be, in no particular order: uplifting, awful, inspiring, regimented, ridiculous and helpful.

Certainly if the behaviours adopted by managers at the away day are radically different from their normal way of dealing with people, the days can often be a complete disaster, with no one quite knowing what the ground rules are. On the other hand, the quality of the time spent may be markedly more conducive to more diffuse and complex approaches.

NOW TRY THIS: Plus, minus, interesting

Try this exercise to see what you think about away days. It's based on an idea of Edward de Bono's.

Use these headings to decide on what you think is good (Plus), and bad (Minus) about away days. Then move on to a third category, things that are neither good nor bad, just interesting. De Bono suggests that it is often in this third category that you are most creative.

Plus	*Minus*	*Interesting*

■ The need for fruitful disorder

What does your desk look like at work? What about at home? Or are these desks one and the same for you? Does it look different when you are in the middle of some kind of project? Is it tidy? Hopelessly messy? Can you find things when you need them, like a squirrel retrieving a nut stored in the autumn? Or is it more like a dog searching for a bone buried in some half-remembered spot in the garden of your mind? How do you capture your own good ideas so that they do eventually turn into lightbulbs?

And how tidy and abstract do you like your own information to be? Do you insist that information and ideas come to you in well argued and graphically pleasing prose? Or do you like to pick up impressions and ideas on the hoof, even though they may not form a coherent pattern yet? Do you like to hear what real people are really thinking and worrying about? Or do you prefer spreadsheets and simulated projections under a range of growth assumptions?

There are stories of the Body Shop's Anita and Gordon Roddick's weekly 'board walk': a formalized attempt to hear from the grassroots what was going on in all departments of the business. And Intel's phenomenally successful CEO Andrew Grove was convinced of the greater value of informal information over elegant reports. 'The type of information most useful to me, and I suspect most useful to all managers, comes from quick, often casual conversational exchanges, many of them on the telephone,' he said. Written reports, Grove argued, were much more useful to the writer than the reader. The discipline of writing a report, especially during the elaboration and evaluation phase of a project, forced you to think more clearly. For the author, it may be time well spent. For the reader, it may equally well be a waste of time.

Many creative people talk of the fine balance that exists between chaos and order, neatness and mess. Too neat and there is no space for flexibility. Too messy and it is impossible to operate effectively. You need a kind of fruitful disorder to give full rein to your creativity in both your personal life and more organizationally at work.

Dee Hock, ex-CEO of the mighty Visa corporation, believes that creative organizations need to be less rigid. He coined a new word to seek to capture the essence of a fluid modern organization: 'chaordic'. As he describes it: 'I borrowed the first syllable of each [word – order and chaos], combined them and chaord (kayord) emerged. By chaord, I mean any self-organizing, self-governing, adaptive, nonlinear, complex organism, organization, community or system, whether physical, biological or social, the behaviour of which harmoniously blends characteristics of both chaos and order. Loosely translated to business, it can be thought of as an organization that harmoniously blends characteristics of competition and cooperation; or from the perspective of education, an organization that seamlessly blends theoretical and experiential learning.'

Another term, 'adhocracy' (from 'ad hoc' and 'bureaucracy'), also seeks to capture this essence of fruitful disorder. Emerging from the total quality management (TQM) movement to describe an organization that is the antithesis of a bureaucracy, there is some uncertainty as to whether it was first coined by Warren Bennis or by Alvin Toffler. It matters not. The term has now been popularized by Robert Waterman, who defines it as 'any form of organization that cuts across normal bureaucratic lines to capture opportunities, solve problems, and get results'. Buzzword or not, adhocracy somehow captures the spirit of untrammelled individual creativity and fluidity necessary to allow ideas to flourish.

Creating flexible systems

To implement ideas you need systems, but if the systems are too rigid they are likely to put creative people off using them. Order supports hard thinking, but a degree of disorder encourages softer, more diffuse approaches.

An example of a good, flexible system is the one that Julian Richer, the founding CEO of Richer Sounds, set up. This enabled managers to take all of their teams out for a drink once a month and spend £5 on each of them. The results of this simple system were improved morale, increased trust and better informal communication between staff.

A similarly positive environment is created by South West Airlines when they give each employee one week away from work each year to develop ideas that might be of value to the business.

These are just two minor examples of creative systems. At a macro level, it is possible to see changing practices too. Many companies now regard the three-year business plan as 'old hat'. An organization needs a vision, short-term goals and the operating systems that are going to deliver the strategy, but trying to tie everything down in words and figures may be counter-productive. Plans produced in a rolling cycle are more helpful than those set in stone for a number of years. You are increasingly likely to find rough guides rather than detailed manuals in creative organizations.

As we focus more and more on the way organizations do things, we are really talking about organizational culture, or, as Gareth Morgan puts it: 'How organizations behave when no one is looking'. Ultimately it is in these moments that it is possible to see into the soul of an organization and determine just how much fruitful disorder it can tolerate!

■ Counter-creative communication

We started this chapter by talking about ecology. The plants you choose, we asserted, are critically important to the habitats that you end up creating.

The workplace equivalent to plants is, surely, language. For it is in language that the creative eco-system is embedded – the creatogenic environment that you need to secure for yourself and those with whom you work.

Powerpoint

We have seen how counter-productive certain kinds of powerpoint presentation can be. In-built to its templates are the dreaded bullet points. These mysterious triffids of contemporary punctuation exert their dread influence over people's thinking processes. Where a heading deserves no amplification or at best, perhaps, one further clarifying thought, you suddenly find three or four meaningless bullet points appearing. The structure of the template and the language it engenders ensure that creativity is stifled or bored to death. Sometimes the most important thing that creative people can do is to avoid a particular means of communication.

Emails

Many emails exert a similarly destructive force on creativity. Their stealthy replicability, aided by the 'copy to' button, ensure that we are deluged with nonsense or corporate spam. Unlike in the early days of faxes, when people would often assume that it had not got through and send a hard copy back-up, emailers blithely assume that once sent it has effectively been read. Of course this could not be further from the truth. It may be stuck in cyber space or more likely sitting on the electronic equivalent of the doormat, in a steady queue. Once upon a time it used to be fun to return from a holiday to discover your piles of mail. These days such experiences are the daily nightmare of switching on your email. We have already seen how, to be creative, you need a bit of space. Mounting piles of emails somehow manage to encroach on the mind of even the most robust of individuals. Creative people have strategies for deleting many of them without even reading them and limiting the amount of time spent on the ones they want to read. Here is a neat tip we encountered recently. When you are on leave, leave an auto-reply message that says: 'I am away until such and such date. I shall not be reading any emails sent to me during this period, so, if your message is really important, please re-send it again after such and such date.' Or you can simply decide to delete without reading any email where you do not recognize either the sender or the subject.

The nadir of e-communication was reached in 2003, when a number of companies sacked individuals, and in one example the whole workforce, by sending them a text message on their phones.

James Dyson, inventor and successful British entrepreneur, is a good example of someone who knows just how wasteful of creativity emails can be. He discourages both emails *and* memos in his company. Many emails are, in fact, memos. And the thing about memos is that they tend to be one-way communication of the 'I am going to tell you something that I need to get off my chest' variety. In an early Harry Potter story by J.K. Rowling, there is a wonderful moment in the Ministry of Magic: 'Several paper aeroplanes swooped into the lift. Harry stared at them as they flapped idly around above his head. "Just interdepartmental memos," Mr Weasley muttered to him. "We used to use owls but the mess was unbelievable."' The image of memos flapping idly about our heads and dropping their verbal guano on the office floor is an enduring one.

◼ Using the power of language

'She was afraid because of the power of these words, which affected her so strongly, who had nothing to do with what they stood for.'

Doris Lessing

Here are five ways in which the detail of the language you choose to use is important.

The present tense

The first is in the use of the present tense when talking about experiences. It is smart to use this sparingly, because it implies a permanence which can easily lead to rigidity. So if you say, 'I am no good at this' or 'I cannot think of a way of doing that', you slip into a linguistic trap that can all too easily lead to a negative view of yourself and of the world. It is what Martin Seligman calls 'learned pessimism'. You begin to assume that things are against you. A simple shift into the past tense will release you to think fresh thoughts about the situation. 'I am no good at this' becomes 'I wasn't good at this then' or 'I used not to be much good at this, but now…'.

NOW TRY THIS: Past-tensing

Go into your relaxed mode. Think of all the things that are on your mind at the moment. Let them gently fill your mind. Which of them are troubling you? You could go back to the bug list you created on page 40 if you need to jog your memory.

Create some present-tense sentences to describe some of these. 'I do not seem to be able to…', 'I am worried about…' and so on. As each of these sentences comes into your mind, imagine that it is a thing of the past.

Say it out loud.

Now tell your mind to consign it to your memory and, as you do so, think of another sentence using a verb in the past tense, 'I used to be worried about…, but now…'

Repeat these sentences out loud.

Scour your mind for as many present-tense 'demons' as you can…

After a while scribble some of these thoughts down on a piece of paper.

You could make two columns, one headed 'Present', one 'Past'.

Tone of voice

The second concerns the way you say things. Compare these two pieces of advice:

'You need to change the way you run your meetings.'

'You might like to consider starting the meeting by quickly asking each of those present to share what is on their mind.'

Which piece of advice would you prefer to receive? Most people opt for the second one. The reason for this is that, whereas the first one seems to be a command, the second is much gentler, offering a suggested way ahead while at the same time leaving you the creative freedom to accept the suggestion or do something different.

The more you can create a world of creative possibility, the better people will perform. Tone matters, too, acting as a kind of corporate laxative!

Real contexts

Allied to this is our third observation. Not only is tone significant, so is context. For example, many people find it easier to relate to real people in real (if imagined) contexts than they do to relate to abstract ideas. Try the following exercise, which is based on a puzzle invented by psychologist Peter Wason.

NOW TRY THIS: Vowels or drinks?

Four cards on a table are labelled A, B, 3 and 4. Each card has a letter on one side and a number on the other. Any card with a vowel on it always has an even number on the other side. Which cards do you have to turn over to be able to say whether this rule is true or false?

Or try this version of the same problem. Imagine that four people are drinking in a bar. One person is drinking coke. One is 16 years old. One is drinking beer. One is 18 years old. Given the rule that you need to be older than 18 in Britain to drink alcohol, which of the drinkers do you need to check to see if the law is being observed?

Which of these did you find easiest to solve? Most people find the second one much easier, and, although both of these questions are essentially the same, many people find the first one impossible to solve. (Solutions on page 195.)

In the context of the workplace this is very important. It would seem to suggest that many people are simply not able to give of their creative best because they cannot relate to the language being used. It may be as simple as avoiding the use of acronyms or technical jargon or as complex as making sure that you reframe problems in a number of different ways so that the fullest possible range of brains is engaged in seeking to solve them.

The brain's love of patterns

The fourth takes us from verbs to nouns, adjectives and adverbs. It concerns the brain's love of patterns. We love to organize data into logical sections. We create dictionaries to organize thousands of words so we can retrieve them alphabetically. We name streets so that we will not get lost in cities. And in the workplace we label departments (finance, back office, marketing, and so on) and jobs (managers, teachers, cleaners, for example). In short, we give things names so that we can remember how they fit into the scheme of things. We classify people and functions (smart, in a support role, for example). We even classify ideas (good, wacky, interesting, bad, and so on).

Efficient and helpful as this classifying tendency may be, it is also dangerous, as language expert James Britton puts it: 'We classify at our peril. Experiments have shown that even the lightest touch of the classifier's hand is likely to induce us to see members of a class as more alike that they actually are and items from different classes as less alike than they actually are.' So, as a creative person, hold back from immediately classifying your ideas. Allow some of them to swim around 'unfiled'.

Metaphors

Fifth and finally, metaphors are powerful ways of conveying meaning in increasingly prosaic working environments. Metaphors combine thought and emotion, enriching communication.

The best kinds of brand operate in this way. Juxtaposed with a product is a way of life to which we are invited to connect imaginatively. Advertisements imply levels of meaning and of connectedness. They give us mental models that expand our conception of things. Poet and creative consultant David Whyte has shown how it is possible to bring metaphor and poetry into the workplace as an aid to creativity. So, for example, in his book *The Heart Aroused*, he uses the Anglo-Saxon poem *Beowulf* as a metaphor for today's employee understanding more about power and vulnerability at work. He helps us to explore our own demons just as Beowulf does when he faces dangerous monsters in a far-off world.

Metaphors encourage soft, diffuse, inward thinking as they are capable of many levels of interpretation and sit well alongside our inner-net of memories. Learning to think in metaphors can foster creativity. In nature, for example, there many examples of symbiotic relationships, creatures (often small) which live on other creatures (often larger), each performing a service for the other and helping it to survive. Many organizations are trying to encourage similar relationships with their suppliers and customers. So, if you were to take the metaphor of a symbiotic animal relationship and apply it to your own situation at work, you might gain other insights as a consequence.

Sometimes metaphors grow into stories. So business leaders talk about the values which led to the formation of their company and of how employees struggled and overcame tough situations to produce remarkable results. Creative people often use stories to engage those with whom they are working. What about you? Do you use stories when you are working with colleagues?

Of course the vast majority of our ideas, hunches and insights at work are tacit or implicit. They may not even have been put into words. Sometimes the soft-sensing approaches that we discussed earlier are necessary to let the patterned information that is there emerge from a single complex scene. But often the pattern – and the ability to predict and control the situation that goes with it – only emerges over time, from looking cumulatively at a range of experiences. Psychologists refer to this phenomenon as 'implicit learning': implicit, because the information that accrues manifests itself only in the way you intuitively act, and is not available to conscious analysis. You 'know', but you do not know how you know.

■ Avoid the cynicism trap

An environment that has been secured for the purposes of encouraging people to be creative needs a commitment to innovation from the top. Although this sounds obvious, innovation founders when there is a difference between the rhetoric and the reality of an organization's approach to creativity. If there is a lot of hype about being a 'learning organization' or an innovative company, but no follow-through, the culture quickly becomes cynical.

Cynicism is death to creativity and innovation, because it robs people of their enthusiasm. If they are encouraged to come up with good ideas which then languish for lack of support, they are not going to be so keen to bother in the future. Sometimes managers want to look and sound innovative, but then fail to put their money where their mouth is.

As we have seen, the processes of developing and implementing ideas is often a lengthy and uncertain one: managers should have a realistic idea of what they are taking on, and not promise more than they can deliver. It is better to invite less in the way of creative participation and to honour what comes, than to make sweeping statements, which are then, tacitly or openly, retracted or shrunk, while people's contributions get brushed aside.

Making time for creative thought

Talk to many successful innovators about why they did something and they will often simply tell you that they had a hunch they were on to something.

One of the ways in which a positive environment can be fostered is through a relaxed but purposeful attitude to time. When there are moments of great activity it is equally important that there is some down-time. In short, you need to find your own rhythms of pressure and ease at work.

At 3M this means allocating 15 per cent of time to employees for the purpose of ideas generation. In a number of consultancies, it involves giving employees time out after especially demanding assignments.

In many organizations, time is short, and much hangs on the outcomes of innovation. There are real pressures and risks: jobs, reputations, sales, examination results, even the survival of the organization itself. So talk of leisurely exploration has to be embedded within a context that is often, and rightly, hard-headed and time-limited. But as we have seen throughout this book, the call for time and space to ruminate is not born of nostalgia for a slower world. It comes from the scientifically validated recognition that if you want people to come up with good ideas, it is pragmatically smart to allow them to intermingle hard with soft thinking, and concentrated with diffused modes of awareness.

The joy of flexible workstyles

'Work used to mean things that we had to do, or were paid to do, usually for other people. Now it increasingly also means things that we choose to do. That little shift makes all the difference. For one thing, it means that no one need ever be out of work. They may be out of money, but that is less demoralizing than having nothing to do, and, actually easier to do something about.'

Charles Handy

Both of us work from home. We are portfolio workers, using our minds for a variety of different clients. Sometimes we write, like now. Other times we may be advising a business or a school or a government department. We sell our ideas and know-how, either in person or on the page. Unless we are out working with clients, our working environment is also, therefore, our home environment. We, and people like us, have no excuses if we do not seek to arrange our environment to be most conducive to the development of our creativity.

Charles Handy has been an inspiration for many portfolio workers in that he showed with great skill and great modesty how you can be a flea in an age of corporate elephants. Small is fun. Self-employment is a real option, not just for those who have traditionally sold their services in this way like plumbers and electricians, but for a much wider section of society.

We are part of a growing number of people globally who, with the advent of technology and with a shift in patterns of employment, no longer believe in job-shaped jobs. We are independent of the traditional employment relationship. We recently sat in a room of forty- and fifty-somethings. Seventy-five per cent of us were portfolio workers. Maybe we hang out with similar people and should expect this. But ten years ago to be a portfolio worker was unusual. Today it is accepted. The Office of National Statistics reports that in 2000 there were 2.2 million self-employed people in the UK.

According to a survey in *Management Today* in 2003, 32 per cent of people would prefer homeworking because:

There's no commute	44 per cent
It's a better environment	17 per cent
It's more productive	16 per cent
It's quiet and peaceful	8 per cent
Other reasons	15 per cent

But it may not be for everyone. Valerie Bayliss, author of *Redefining Work*, a research project undertaken by the Royal Society of Arts, puts it like this: 'People will move, over time, back and forth along a work spectrum. There will still be conventional, "job-shaped" jobs, but run much more like self-employed jobs are now. For most of us, work will take an almost infinite variety of forms. Flexible working patterns will dominate. The idea of a private sector career, or a public sector career, or a career in a single skill, will have disappeared. Conventional boundaries between private, public and voluntary sectors will have broken down.'

A good example of flexible working is the system adopted by Kellog, Brown and Root, which enables all their employees to work a nine-day week, routinely taking a long weekend every other week by the simple expedient of working slightly longer hours on each of the nine days. Morale has risen considerably, and so, we would suggest, has creativity.

NOW TRY THIS: In a perfect world

Have you ever stopped to think why certain jobs are done from an office or a fixed point? Why, for example, do you go to a lawyer in their office while a life insurance salesperson will often be prepared to come to your home? Why do you go to school rather than school coming to you? Or go to a library rather than it coming to you? (You can perhaps see where we are going, because in these examples things are already changing.)

Think of all the jobs you can. You might like to do this by chatting to a colleague or friend. Where do they currently take place? Invent a way for each one to be undertaken in a different location. Now think about your own situation. Where do you currently go to work? Where else could work like yours be done? Where would you like to do it?

Dream on. It might just happen!

Flexibility of environment is important, just as flexibility of thought, approach and mindset is. So if the structure of the environment is too rigid, creativity is unlikely to flourish, as Jack Welch, CEO of General Electric, has made abundantly clear: 'Hierarchy is an organization with its face towards the CEO and its ass towards the customer.'

In the final chapter of *The Creative Thinking Plan*, we return to the pressures, complexities and opportunities of modern life and see how 'well-being' and 'creativity' are interconnected. We look at the ways in which you can look after yourself to ensure that you are in peak condition physically to be mentally creative.

Solutions from page 190
The A card and the 3 card   The beer drinker and the 16-year-old

Learn to listen to your body
and find out what it thinks

Chapter 8
Healthy body, creative mind

○ Change perspective

○ Keep a journal

○ Focus on your feelings

○ Breathe with all your muscles

○ Know your emotional patterns

○ Talk honest nonsense

○ Nurture the body–mind connection

'Annual income twenty pounds, annual expenditure nineteen and six, result happiness.'

Mr Micawber in David Copperfield, *by Charles Dickens*

If only it were so simple! Enough money (and enough time) = happy creativity! We started this book by looking at conducive habits of mind and we end it by doing the same for your body. For if you are going to stay creative you will need to balance the conflicting demands of work and home and make sure that you are healthy. This will involve looking after your body and being responsive to its needs, along with some common-sense practical steps.

■ Being 'in sorts'

At the micro level, we just need to get better at being 'in sorts'. We all know what it is like to be out of sorts. But, as Daniel Goleman has shown in his book *Emotional Intelligence*, it is possible to alter your mental and emotional state, repairing your mood so that you ensure that you are in sorts. Creativity in all walks and departments of life is significantly enhanced if we get smarter about our own emotional patterns and the bear-traps we habitually fall into.

You know that if you are trying to work and you get sleepy, it can help to open a window, or do some quick exercises, or splash cold water on your face. By the same token, if you are feeling fed up and out of sorts, you know that it might help to shift the energy if you call up a friend, or go for a brisk walk. So if you are too agitated to be able to drop into your reverie state, do whatever you know to do in order to reduce the agitation. If it is a simple problem, deal with it. Put the garbage out. Make that awkward phone call. If not, do what you can to calm yourself down – listen to music, stroke the cat – in a way that does not lose the 'alert' part of the mind – that is, not by drinking yourself into a stupor!

Humour is conducive to balance. Finding something that will put you in a good mood, when you need to think well, is a good idea. Arthur Koestler, in *The Act of Creation*, points out how closely allied are humour and creativity. They both feed on the same state of mind. It is hard to see the funny side or to take part in the banter if you are worried or uptight. Studies by Alice Isen and colleagues at the University of Maryland have shown that people who have just watched a five-minute film clip of bloopers are more than five times as likely to solve a problem requiring creative thinking as people who have not. You can check this out for yourself the next time you have a difficulty to resolve with family or colleagues. Start the meeting with a joke or a funny anecdote and see if lightening the mood results in more creative approaches by all concerned. (Humour is an individual thing – but here's a favourite joke of ours. An elephant was walking through the jungle when he caught sight of a mouse. 'My!' he said. 'You are small.' 'I know,' said the mouse. 'I've not been well.')

■ The work–life debate

'I am trying to cultivate a lifestyle that does not require my presence.'

Garry Trudeau

How do you react to this information, produced as part of a major exploration of working life undertaken by universities in Britain?

Per cent of people completely or very satisfied with hours worked

	Men		Women	
	1992	*2000*	*1992*	*2000*
Higher level professionals and managers	36	16	38	26
Lower level professionals and managers	33	18	44	28
Higher admin/clerical/sales	38	33	58	35
Technical/supervisors	29	20	45	17
Skilled manual	39	22	44	17
Semi and unskilled manual	34	15	57	22

These statistics suggest to us that there has been a considerable decline in job satisfaction mainly because of the hours that people are now required to work. Jonathon Porritt, chairman of the UK Sustainable Development Commission, launched a stinging attack on the prevailing economic model of endless growth: 'We can no longer depend on our growth-obsessed model of progress to generate the improvements in quality of life and personal well-being that people are so hungry for.' Or, as David Whyte puts it in *The Heart Aroused*: 'The rich flow of creativity, innovation and almost musical complexity we are looking for in a fulfilled life cannot be reached through trying or working harder.'

Being creative contributes to a happy life. It is about working and living smarter rather than harder or longer. Of course success is necessary for self-esteem, but there are ways of achieving it other than having your job title on the door of your office. By the same token, job roles need not define our identity. You are a parent first and a doctor second, or a guitar player more than you are an electrician, and so on. It is possible to develop ways of working that are more likely to enable you to live the creative life. More flexible working patterns, periods of unpaid leave, the provision of childcare and the use of technology for home-working are just four examples.

According to the UK Work Foundation, the benefits to business of work–life balance include increased productivity, improved recruitment and retention and lower rates of absenteeism – in short, a more motivated, satisfied, creative and equitable workforce.

The drift of many of these initiatives is to reduce working hours and enable people to spend more time with their families. Although, as George Burns said: 'Happiness is having a large, loving, caring, close-knit family in another city.' Families do not suit everyone. For some people, work is a relief from home!

NOW TRY THIS: Life meets work

A very practical way of moving beyond the rhetoric of the phrase 'work–life balance' is to hold a series of meetings in your workplace to come up with ways of improving it.

You could start each one with a shortened form of the relaxation exercise you have been using to get people in the right mindset. And perhaps you could try out some different techniques for generating ideas.

Most importantly you should be able to begin to do some things more creatively than you have done them in the past.

■ Varying perspectives help memory

If you love work and hate home, then you will not want to rush home. What about if you enjoy work and enjoy home? Or if you like working in short, hard bursts and then chilling out? Everyone is different and everyone has a different view of balance. Forty hours a week may be twenty hours too many for some and barely enough to get started for others. It all depends on how you see the world.

Remember the puzzle about the candle on page 165? Once you took a different view of the box it suddenly became clear how to create a shelf. Or, with the two ropes puzzle on page 83, once you viewed an ordinary object as a weight to be attached to one of the ropes and mentally got the rope swinging, it all fell into place.

People who are less able, or less inclined, to constrain their interpretations of details to fit in with their overall sense of the context, tend to see those details more clearly, and this is a mixed blessing. Autistic people are often handicapped in everyday life by their tendency to see the 'trees' but not the 'forest'. But the fact that some have the ability to execute incredibly detailed drawings is well known. And, freed to a degree from the pressure to find overall coherence, they are also sometimes able to see more creatively.

Francesca Happé, a psychologist in London, tells the story of an autistic child she was testing by asking him questions about a doll's bedroom containing miniature furniture. 'What's that?' she asked, pointing first at the bed and then at the blanket. The child named the items 'correctly'. 'And that?' she asked, pointing at the small pillow, covered in a little pillowcase with a scalloped edge. 'A piece of ravioli,' said the boy – and indeed that is exactly what it looked like. Perhaps he was able to see with some of the clarity and freshness of vision that Rodin and Cézanne were laboriously seeking through their 'staring'.

Variety helps, too. Ellen Langer offered student volunteers a free piano lesson. Two groups both practised a simple C-major scale, but one was instructed to do so using as many different variations as they could. 'Try to change your style every few minutes, and not lock into one particular pattern,' they were told. The other group just tried to play the scale as well as they could. The efforts of both groups were taped and evaluated by two experienced pianists. The group who had learnt with variation was rated as more competent and creative in their playing. They also said they had enjoyed the lesson more.

Variation also improves memory. Groups of adults read short stories during their commuter train journeys, and some of them were also asked to imagine the events in the stories from the perspectives of different characters, or to think up different endings. When they were tested for their memory, the variation group recalled many more details than people who had read the stories straight. When tenth-grade students took part in a similar experiment, those who had read a story from different perspectives recalled more, and also showed more creativity, and insight into the stories, in the essays they subsequently wrote.

Even after the event, memory is improved by trying to recall a story from the perspective of different actors. For example, some people were given an inventory of the contents of a house to study, and were later asked to recall as many items as they could. When they had run out, they were asked to imagine the house from the perspective first of the householder, and secondly of a burglar. As each new perspective was added, so they were able to gain access to some more of the items that had previously been inaccessible. Insights such as these have had a practical influence on the way police interview prospective witnesses. In the widely used 'cognitive interview technique', witnesses' memories are jogged by asking them to try to recall events from someone else's point of view.

So, when it comes to organizing your life, variety is key. You could take different routes to work, do different things in the evening, cook different meals for supper and so on, and regardless of the amount of time you spend at work, your life might seem more balanced.

One variation that seems particularly important is whether learning is construed as 'work' or 'play'. Adults were given a calendar of Gary Larson's *Far Side* cartoons and asked to sort them in various ways that were more or less interesting or challenging. For half the participants, these activities were described as 'play'; for the other half they were referred to as 'work'. Particularly on the more challenging tasks, people who thought they were 'playing' rated the activities as more enjoyable, and reported that their minds wandered only half as often, as those who saw themselves as 'working'. When we call something 'work', it often locks people into the idea that they have to come up with the 'best' or the 'correct' solution, and this both narrows their cone of attention (to what they think 'they' want), and increases performance anxiety

This has all sorts of obvious implications for the notion of work–life balance. And the most obvious of these is the way you choose to think of the different parts of your life. If you can think of work, either totally or partially, as play and actively seek ways of taking control of elements of it so that you can do it in your own way, it may seem more creative to you. Who knows, the next time you are asked to do the washing-up, you could volunteer enthusiastically with a knowing smile on your face as you determine to treat it all as a game.

With this kind of approach, rules suddenly become things to be subverted or enjoyed rather than irritated by. Think of the marvellously tongue-in-cheek ones that Mark Twain gives us at the start of *The Adventures of Huckleberry Finn*: 'Persons attempting to find a motive in this narrative will be prosecuted; persons attempting to find a moral in it will be banished; persons attempting to find a plot in it will be shot. By order of the author.'

NOW TRY THIS: Turning rules into opportunities

Think of the three rules in your working life that most irritate you. Take a moment to write them down.

Now do a Huckleberry Finn on them. Have some fun with them. Add some humour or tweak them so that they sound ironic. Make them say the opposite of what they seem to saying. Take them to their logical conclusion and see what happens.

■ Taking life decisions

'When you have to make a choice and don't make it, that is in itself a choice.'

William James

As you seek to live a creative life, you will inevitably be faced with tough decisions. How will you go about taking them? Hundreds of consumer magazines and websites exist today. Their purpose is to convince us that there is a reason to buy one product rather than another one. One is more environment-friendly, another costs less, the third contains more stuff per packet, and so on. You could easily think that consumer decisions are largely rational. Why is it that so many people read horoscopes with more than mild interest on a regular basis? Do you rely on astrology? Do you only currently heed hard facts? Try this exercise to get a true picture of the way you go about deciding things.

NOW TRY THIS: Understanding your own decision-making processes

What is the most important decision you have made in your life so far? Close your eyes and let your mind relax. Think back over your life to date. What floats up? A decision to start or end a relationship? The moment when you decided to buy your house? Your decision to take a certain job?

Whatever comes to mind, focus on it for a moment.

'Walk round it' for a bit.

What did it feel like?

What effect has it had on you?

Who helped you to decide?

How did you go about deciding?

Did you rely on your heart or your head or a bit of both?

Many of your most important decisions involve intuition. The house feels right. The person who is offering you the job seems a nice guy. You fall in love, and so on. You almost expect them to have an intuitive element. You decide without consciously deciding. As author Robert Keith Leavitt puts it: 'People don't ask for facts in making up their minds. They would rather have a good soul-satisfying emotion than a dozen facts.'

It is similar for many small daily actions that take place automatically. You decide which word to use depending on who you are with. You make connections between the behaviour of a colleague and other things going on that you are only dimly aware of. You infer the likely weather from clues in the atmosphere. This kind of processing is what Arthur Reber calls 'primitive', that is, the basic elements of our survival.

Contrast this with a more 'sophisticated' processing that involves you in accessing your inner-net of experiences to use in more complex decisions (of the kind you were conjuring up in the last exercise you did). This is the kind of decision-making that you need to use on a more regular basis. It is slower. It allows you, when under pressure, not to go for the first solution. It helps you to avoid being stereotypical, to absorb the full range of data and be deep and broad in your analysis. But you know about all this from earlier chapters.

■ Developing a store of your experiences

'The journal is the larder of reflexive intelligence.'

Peter Abbs

At the heart of living the creative life is self-knowledge. In a fast-moving world things change so fast that reflecting on your inner voices and giving vent to your hunches and emotions are all really important.

Keeping a journal

One of the best strategies for cultivating all these attitudes and skills is the keeping of a journal or a 'commonplace book'. Stray thoughts, observations and quotations that inspire you, puzzle you, pique your interest or annoy you intensely can be captured and frozen on a page, where they can be revisited and mulled over, to see what they might mean or where they might lead, and to feed your imagination at a later date.

At the time of his death, Thomas Edison had filled 3,400 notebooks, each of 200 pages, with his musings, jottings and observations. In the middle of a meal or a conversation, he'd whip out his journal to note down a phrase or an intruding memory that had, on the spur of the moment, as one of his biographers put it, 'jogged up a technological possibility'.

Developing this habit of collecting stray thoughts also sharpens your ability to see them. You become more on the lookout for interesting bits and pieces, and more acute at spotting and holding on to them. 'A man should learn to detect and watch that gleam of light which flashes across his mind from within, more than the lustre of the firmament of bards and sages,' said Ralph Waldo Emerson.

Sociologist C. Wright Mills says of 'accomplished thinkers', that: 'the reason they treasure their smallest experiences is that… experience is so important as a source of original intellectual work.' A great fan of the notebook, Mills also sees it as an aid to being simultaneously respectful and quizzical towards one's own experience. 'To be able to trust yet to be sceptical of your own experience, I have come to believe, is one mark of the mature workman,' he says. 'This ambiguous confidence is indispensable to originality in any intellectual pursuit, and the file [notebook] is one way by which you can develop and justify such confidence.'

The emphasis on recording your lived experience is also important for it serves as a fertile source of ideas for all kinds of creative projects: professional, artistic, playful and intellectual. When you stay too closely within one expert domain, your ideas can become stale and incestuous, feeding on the minutiae of technical disputes rather than being grounded in and continually refreshed by your own felt interests and concerns. If you work as an industrial research chemist, it may be hard to see how your day-to-day work in the laboratory can be much infused with your personal passions, but not so if you are an architect, or a schoolteacher, or a journalist, or a nurse, or a social scientist.

■ Talk honest nonsense

You can often think more creatively if you are not at the same time trying to record your thoughts in your Sunday-best prose style, or even handwriting, come to that. So don't worry about style. As Socrates said to Callistos: 'Sometimes when you've been trying really hard to get a glimpse of an idea you can only talk about it in a kind of nonsense. So stop trying to be clear, and just talk honest nonsense.'

As you begin to understand yourself more fully and as you begin to put into your life the approaches we have been describing in *The Creative Thinking Plan*, it is almost inevitable that you will understand more about how you are actually *different* from other people.

As George Bernard Shaw suggests, this may well be a sign that you are on to something: 'The reasonable man adapts himself to the world; the unreasonable one persists in trying to adapt the world to himself. Therefore all progress depends on the unreasonable man.' You may have to persist with your family and work colleagues to persuade them that it is worth adopting the approaches that you are suggesting.

■ Sensing the body–mind connection

'The distinction between mind and body is an artificial dichotomy, a discrimination which is unquestionably based far more on the peculiarity of intellectual understanding than on the nature of things.'

Carl Jung

You have already seen some of the ways in which your heart and your mind are connected through your emotions. The same is true of your body. Tradition has it that mind and body somehow inhabit different worlds, only coming together at moments of crisis. At a time of personal disaster, such as the loss of a family member or a divorce, we might succumb to illness as a result of the stress. But the assumption that mind and body are intimately connected is rarely part of our day-to-day lives. We do not, as a matter of course, see the links between the health of our minds and that of our bodies. You need to listen to the inner promptings of your body in the same way you strain to catch glimpses of your intuition.

One practical way of becoming more aware of your body is consciously to explore your senses. Try this exercise as a way of reminding you of the full glorious 'sound' of them when they are in action.

NOW TRY THIS: The multimedia symphony

Sit quietly and relaxed where you will not be disturbed.

Open your eyes
When you open your eyes try to include all the senses in your momentary awareness – so that you are appreciating the multimedia symphony – the *son et lumière* and all the other senses – that is going on every moment. Don't look around to start with. Just gaze into space. What do you see? Are you labelling and dissecting, or can you see the scene in soft focus? Can you move between the two extremes? Include the senses of touch and smell… What body sensations are you experiencing? How is your skin? Are there any smells? Now can you put the different senses together?

Try this outside
Stand in the open. Feel the wind on your skin. Sniff the breeze. See the branches of the trees swaying. Listen to the rustle of the leaves… Now can you do that all at once? See if you can let your sensory doors be flung wide open all at the same time, and allow yourself to be flooded by the total experience. If you find it hard, keep practising in odd moments. You will get flashes of it to start with, and then with a bit more practice, you'll be able to switch more on at will. In a meeting, see if you can suddenly switch out of your intellectual mode – following the discussion; having private

thoughts, reactions and judgement; thinking about what to say and how to get your way – and experience the scene just as a sensory symphony for a few seconds. (It can be refreshing, and amusing.)

◾ Tuning in to your physical responses

'I feel therefore I am.'

Robert Witkin

Human beings are not computers. While there are some ways in which this metaphor is useful, there are many in which it is not. Computers do not have intrinsic needs and wants. You can programme a robot to seek a certain goal, but it does not shrivel up and die if it does not get it. You could take out the 'brain' and the 'memory' of my computer and put it into a hundred different kinds of 'body', and it would not turn a hair. In human beings, the 'central processor' of the brain is much more intimately tied up with the 'peripherals' of the body, and with the set of biological and social pressures that the body–brain system as a whole has evolved to cope with.

The knowledge stored in the brain reaches back down the sensory pathways, modulating and guiding the way they behave. The eyes and the brain are so closely interconnected through feedback and feed-forward loops that they effectively comprise a single system. So do the brain and the other senses. And so too do the brain and the heart; the brain and the respiratory system; the brain and the endocrine system which controls emotion; the brain and the immune system. All the different organs of the body are bound together much more tightly than we used to think. Now we know that they communicate immediately and extensively via direct neural connections, through our hormones and through chemical messengers called peptides. What we see and hear, and what we are thinking, has an almost instantaneous physical effect on what is happening in the cells of the stomach wall and the muscles of the diaphragm. Communication between brain and immune system is so close that endocrinologist Candace Pert refers to the immune system as 'a bit of brain floating round the body'.

It is no surprise, therefore, that you can know through your body as well as through your senses and your mind. As your physical and emotional feelings are so intimately influenced by what is happening elsewhere in the body, they provide another vital channel through which you may become conscious of what is going on 'behind the scenes'. 'By the pricking of my thumbs, something evil this way comes,' said one of the witches in Macbeth, and in everyday language you talk about a gut feeling, or a feeling in your bones.

The poet and scholar A.E. Housman was once asked to define 'poetry', to which he replied:

'… I could no more define poetry than a terrier could define a rat, but that I thought that we both recognize the object by the physical symptoms which it provokes in us… Experience has taught me, when I am shaving of a morning, to keep watch over my thoughts, because, if a line of poetry strays into my memory, my skin bristles so that the razor ceases to act.'

He went on to describe the physical 'symptoms' poetry could produce: a shiver down the spine; a 'constriction of the throat and a precipitation of water to the eyes'; and another, seated in the pit of the stomach, which 'goes through me like a spear'.

Learning body talk

We have to expand our sense of the 'inner-net' to include our bodies as well as our brains and our unconscious minds. And our physical emotions are often more informative about the activities of the inner-net, and what interpretations are being formed and what plans are being laid there, than your direct mental impressions. You may not consciously feel angry, yet you notice that your hands have involuntarily balled themselves into fists. You may not be aware of being afraid, yet the sensation in the stomach, as you wake to another stressful day, tells a different story. When you are 'full' of emotion – it could as well be pride or happiness as sadness – tears spring to your eyes. When you are depressed, your muscles lose tone, your head hangs and your body slumps.

Recognizing your feelings

Notice too the physical signals that may arise from the effort not to feel. A constriction in the throat may reflect the attempt to damp down tears. An overly measured and polite voice may be symptomatic of the control of anger, with its natural tendency to shout and intimidate. A stiff upper lip prevents a mouth from trembling. Shortness of breath may result from clamping the abdominal muscles to shut off the sensation of anxiety arising from the stomach. Aches and pains of all kinds may reflect chronic tension in muscles that are being clamped in order to suppress the display of some more primary emotion.

What we feel in our bodies is as much a valuable part of our knowing as our thoughts, our inklings and our images. It is smart to be able to tune in to the voice of the body, to allow it to speak, and to heed what it has to say. And you can get better at doing so. Just as with dreams and images, your internal body languages are unique. These examples are common, but each one does not apply to everyone. You have to learn to understand your own signals by paying attention to them, not by studying a manual.

Case Study

George Soros, the Hungarian investor who has made and broken national economies, and amassed a fortune, on the basis of his financial 'instincts', was asked, in his recent book Soros on Soros, *how he knew when to cut his losses when stock markets started to move against him. He replied: 'I feel the pain. I rely a great deal on animal instincts. When I was actively running the fund, I suffered from backache. I used the onset of acute pain as a signal that there was something wrong with my portfolio. The backache didn't tell me what was wrong – you know, lower back for short positions, left shoulder for currencies – but it did prompt me to look for something amiss when I might not have done so otherwise.' Lord Simon, British Industry Minister and ex-Chairman of BP, said, 'Sometimes you don't have to discuss things. You can sense it. The tingle is as important as the intellect.'*

As you seek to realize your creative self, you may want actively to pay more attention to the promptings of your body, noting when they seem to be helpful and getting better at 'reading' them.

Focusing: asking your body what it thinks

This process of asking a question of your body, and then waiting and listening to what it has to say in response, may well feel odd – perhaps very odd, or indeed even totally stupid – at first. But there is a great deal of evidence for its effectiveness as a way of both discovering your questions, and investigating them.

Some of your body sensations and emotions are clear or strong. You don't have any difficulty recognizing when you have stubbed a toe, are feeling nauseous, or are embarrassed, anxious, frustrated or upset. But others are much more shadowy and elusive. You may be aware of being mildly out of sorts, but not able to pin the feeling down. They are the bodily equivalents of the faint inklings and promptings that we explored earlier on pages 87–94, and you experience these more nebulous sensations mostly in the central part of the body, between stomach and throat. They are the as yet unformed precursors of thoughts, emotions and better defined sensations, vague clouds of feeling before they have crystallized into something recognizable.

Psychotherapist Eugene Gendlin calls these hazy, holistic beginnings a 'felt sense', and he has discovered that learning to tune into a felt sense, and allowing it to develop slowly, can be immensely valuable. Back in the 1970s, Gendlin and his colleagues were analyzing hundreds of hours of tapes of psychotherapy, trying to find out what it was that made the difference between people who were making good progress in therapy, and those who seemed to be going round in circles. They discovered that the people who were doing well were those who were spontaneously making use of the felt sense. If at some points they became aware of this unclear bodily state, and were able to slow down their talking in order to pay attention to it, and to try to find exactly the right words or images to catch its overall sense, then they were likely to make good progress.

Gendlin called this patient, attentive process 'focusing'. By 'focusing' he means the kind of broad awareness that we have been developing throughout this book so far, but gently directed towards the central area of the body. It is 'focused' only in the sense that you gently try to keep it in that area. Gendlin went on to make two more important discoveries.

The first was that focusing could be taught. People who were not instinctively making use of it could be shown how to do so, and they were then able to make better progress in identifying the nub of whatever had brought them to therapy in the first place, and begin to resolve it. And the second was that the knack of focusing was of value to people in their everyday professional and personal lives. They did not have to be 'suffering' from some particularly distressing problem. Focusing could help in sorting out any kind of unclear worry or quandary. Focusing did not have to take place within the context of therapy, with the aid of a skilled professional therapist. People could learn to do it by themselves, or with the gentle support of a friend or family member.

Gendlin summed up focusing like this: 'The body is wiser than all our concepts, for it totals them all, and much more. It totals all the circumstances we sense. We get this totalling if we let a felt sense form in inward space.' When we are busily trying to represent and explain our predicament in the familiar language of the habit map, we often end up with the same old story that does not seem to get us anywhere. But if we are able to allow a general sense of the predicament to resonate slowly with the deeper, more integrated, more elastic web of the inner-net, then we may find that something fresher and more insightful begins to emerge. And one of its prime modes of expression is through the body.

NOW TRY THIS: The sequence of focusing

To teach focusing, the process is often broken down into a sequence of stages; though in practice they often interweave and loop back on each other. The first stage involves relaxing and bringing your awareness into the central area of the body. You go into the quiet, receptive, inward, attentive mood that we have been practising throughout the book. Then you may want to take an inventory of what problems or issues are currently unresolved in your life. In the third stage, you take one of your issues and ask yourself a very general question like: 'What is this whole thing about?' You might choose one of the concerns that just bubbled up in the previous stage, or you could decide beforehand what it is you would like to explore.

Either way, it is useful to make a mental note of any other concerns that drew your attention, and to 'let them know' that you have done so and are willing to come back and give them some focusing time at a later date.

That way you clear the decks inside your body and mind, so that you can focus fully on the issue you have selected, without being distracted by other problems that are clamouring to be heard.

A felt sense of the problem begins to form slowly and hazily. Anything that comes to mind immediately you ask the question, especially if it sounds familiar, or even 'righteous', should be politely acknowledged – and put to one side. It is probably the habit map wanting to tell you how things are for your normal ego perspective.

- Go back to being aware of your body, and be receptive to any little tell-tale signs of 'something' beginning to form there. If it takes 30 seconds or more to form, and if you are not really sure, to start with, if there is anything 'there' or not – that is probably a felt sense.

- Keep your attention softly on it, and be prepared to let it develop in its own time. For example, a partner I was working with in a focusing training workshop said, as the felt sense began to develop: 'I feel sort of scared, but I don't know what of. Inside it's like an animal that's totally alert, ears pricked… it's like something's coming; and some part of me has picked it up and is getting ready for it. But "I" don't know what it is yet.'

- Next, when there is a 'something', ask yourself how you would describe this sense. What word or phrase or image could you find that seems to catch the essence of it? It could even be a sound or a physical gesture: so long as it is not a 'story' or an explanation. Gendlin calls this preliminary symbol the 'handle'. When you have found a handle that feels as if it might be right, check back with the felt sense. 'Is that it? Does that [word, image] really fit? Remember: throughout the whole process, the physical feeling is the authority. If your felt sense says 'No', or 'Partly', or 'Sort of', or even 'I suppose so', go back and see if you can find a handle that fits better. When you get it right, there is usually a positive sign: something in your body eases or shifts. 'Yes! That's how it is.' Then you go back to the (changed) felt sense, and see if it now needs a new handle. Don't rush it.

Just as with the dreams in Chapter 4, your job is to patiently befriend the felt sense and allow it to tell you about itself. Gendlin sometimes says the process is like trying to understand a child who does not have the words to tell you what's wrong. You offer your understanding until you get it right.

- As things develop, you can prod the process very softly with some general questions, provided your curiosity remains patient, respectful and friendly. You can ask: 'Is there *more* to this whole thing?', or 'What is it about this whole thing that is so [handle]?' For example, if your handle was the word 'airless', ask yourself what it is about the whole issue that makes it feel so airless. You might invite the felt sense to tell you what the *crux* of the matter is, or what the issue might need to help it move on. Each time you ask a question, you go back to the body to listen for the answer. Asking the occasional question can give your conscious mind something to do during this process. The clever, questing intellect may not be used to sitting on the sidelines like this, and you have to find a way to stop it getting restless and wanting to butt in.

- Being 'friendly' doesn't mean you have to like what you find. As things develop, people sometimes find that behind a feeling of righteousness or indignation there is a more uncomfortable sense of self-criticism or even shame. You might have thought that the problem was how to fix someone else so they didn't bug you so much, and find out that there is something in you that needs fixing too. But try to hold the attitude that, as pioneering therapist Carl Rogers used to say, 'the facts are friendly'. The more accurately you sense the whole predicament (including your part in it), the more likely you are to find a genuinely satisfying solution. It's like you're listening to yourself in the way you would listen to a close friend who was distressed or perplexed.

- This attitude enables you to keep the right distance from the problem. If you get too close to it, feelings, emotions and opinions about it can suck you in so you can no longer see it clearly as a whole, and you may even be overwhelmed by it. Eugene Gendlin says: 'If you want to know what the soup smells like, it is better not to stick your head in it.' If you find that you are 'inside it', and getting really angry or upset, you need to let the feelings dissipate and cool down somewhat until you feel more OK in yourself again. On the other hand if you are too far away from the issue, it has stopped mattering to you, and you cannot really be interested in what it has to say.

- After a while – a focusing session takes anywhere from a few minutes to about half an hour – you will reach a place where you feel you can stop. You may not have a complete 'solution', but it is likely that you will have made some progress in opening the issue up in a way that feels fresher and more productive than talking to yourself, or someone else, in the normal way. In the final stage, you take a moment to review what has come up, and to 'mark your place' so that you can come back another time. You might ask yourself what you would like to take away from the focusing session, to ponder on or remember.

Ann Weiser Cornell, a focusing trainer, says of focusing with a partner: 'Being listened to often feels to me like I'm in a dark hole in the ground, lifting up rocks. Often under the rocks there are more rocks. I know there's treasure under there somewhere, but I need someone who's standing up outside the hole, who's willing to take each rock as I hand it to them, so my hands will be free to pick up the next one. When you focus with a listener, they are taking the words as they come out and holding them for you, so that you can go on to the next words.'

Note, by the way, that this way of working with bodily feelings and sensations is very different from assuming that your 'gut feelings' have got to be right, or that they are in opposition to, and necessarily better than, ideas that arise from more focused thinking. People sometimes fall into the trap of accepting their 'instinct' uncritically. But, as we have seen, this is like jumping out of the frying pan into the fire. Just because hard thinking has its limitations, that does not mean that intellect is always wrong or 'bad' and intuition is always right or 'good'. The two complement each other; mind and body work together. Even in a process like focusing, the time to review the products of intuition at the end is an opportunity to adopt a more 'reality-orientated' – but still friendly – attitude towards them.

In a similar way, intelligence expert Robert Sternberg has suggested that there is something called practical intelligence. This, as its name implies, is partly an antidote to intellectual intelligence, or IQ as it is perhaps better known. It focuses on the capacity of individuals to get on in life and work, rather than being bookish and good at passing examinations. As he puts it: 'How much a professional knows or where he learned it usually matters less than how he has successfully put that knowledge to use in the practice of his profession – in effect his practical intelligence.'

Interestingly, Sternberg lists various attributes that are about reading your body's signals well. These include picking up non-verbal cues and adapting body posture to ensure effective communication.

NOW TRY THIS: Focusing on an issue with a partner

Particularly when you are learning how to focus, it can be very helpful to do it with a partner. You go through the same stages, but your partner can assist you in keeping track of where you are, and holding the right attitude and distance. The key stages are:

- Relaxing and bringing soft-focus awareness into your body
- Making an inventory of your current issues
- Choosing one to focus on
- Asking what it is all about, and inviting a felt sense to form
- Letting the felt sense develop
- Looking for a 'handle' for the felt sense
- Resonating back and forth between felt sense and handle, letting each develop
- 'Marking your place' and reviewing what has come up.

Your partner can talk you through the relaxation exercise at the beginning. When you have selected an issue to work with, you may give your partner a very brief indication of what it is about (but don't launch into the 'story'). You do not even have to tell them what it is about if you don't want to. You can say: 'This is to do with my trouble around eating,' or even just: 'This is about a habit I'd like to change.' They may then ask you: 'What is this whole thing about?', and wait patiently for your felt sense to form.

As you begin to get a handle, you can talk out loud. Your partner can reflect back to you what you have said, but they should stay very close to the words you actually used, especially if they seem to be important or central. On no account must your partner try to interpret what you have said, or explain it. And they must refrain absolutely from adding in any judgements, reactions or associations of their own. If they have missed what was important, don't be sidetracked: just reiterate what is bubbling up from the felt sense.

If you say: 'I don't know why, but as I think about him I feel sort of upset, and a bit lonely,' your partner might say: 'You're feeling kind of upset, and a little lonely, as you think about him.' Even though this reflection may feel as if it is not doing much, your felt sense will feel 'heard' if they have got it right, and it can help you to identify the 'That's it', or 'That's not quite it' feeling. The listener should keep it simple; reflect particularly words that convey emotion or body sensations, and retain whatever is vague in what you say. If you say: 'I'm feeling frustrated, and I don't know why,' they might reflect: 'You're frustrated about something…'

Try focusing for about ten minutes to start with. Then you can talk with your partner about how it went. And if you want, you can then swap roles.

■ Live healthily and feel happy

'Mens sana in corpore sano.' (A healthy mind in a healthy body.)

Juvenal

Many a school has enshrined its belief in healthy living by adopting the motto from the Latin poet, Juvenal. Certainly a healthy body is important and a time-honoured way of ensuring your health is through exercise and physical movement. There are at least four strands to this thinking, of which the last two are, in many ways, the most interesting.

Chemical effects

Exercise literally helps you ward off diseases of various kinds. A study carried out at Harvard showed that men who shed 2,500 calories a day in aerobic exercise were 28 per cent less likely to develop clinical depression. It turns out that the neurotransmitters norepinephrine, dopamine and serotonin (the essential ingredient of Prozac) seem to be increased by exercise. But it is not just stress that is countered by regular exercise; well-being in general is enhanced. Interestingly, all of this is happening at a time when the amount of sporting activity in schools in the UK and the USA is declining. Cultivating a sense of well-being in itself will not make you creative; but it is an important underpinning to your efforts to stay creative over a long period of time.

Biological effects of exercise

The second strand is biological. According to the Pasteur Institute and others, exercise promotes growth in your brain. The connecting fibres between your brain cells or neurons, known as dendrites and axons, are stimulated into action. There is also some evidence that it affects areas of the brain that are involved in memory. As Susan Greenfield, one of the world's acknowledged authorities on the brain, describes it: 'The brain is very sensitive to what is happening to the body and the more you are interacting and stimulating the circuits of the brain, the more agile are your brain cells.' But at its simplest level, exercise causes the brain's fuel, oxygenated blood, to be more available. It thereby helps it to function more effectively. Many organizations have begun to recognize this fact by introducing 'stretch breaks' into long meetings. Anyone who has driven a car for a long time knows the importance of getting out and similarly rejuvenating the brain. Exercise can undoubtedly trigger ideas.

The effect on our senses

The third element has to do with our senses. We use all five of these to take in data about the world (as you found out in the exercise on page 207). In this way, our bodies are intimately connected with our learning and creativity. Interestingly we can (and often do) absorb information by using our sense of sight and hearing. Fortunately (or unfortunately), we hardly need to get up from our seat or move away from our screen to be able to function like this. Many of us are more active by inclination, preferring the richer data stream afforded us when we are more physical in our interaction with the world. The other three senses – smell, taste and touch – are especially important, providing routes into our inner-net and more creative self which are not always available through our eyes and our ears. And of course you could say that intuition, as we have been finding out in this book, is a kind of sixth sense.

The English Romantic poets were famous for suggesting that, to retain the vigour of our imaginations, we need to seek restorative inspiration from the natural world, drinking deep from mountains, rivers and lakes. Our senses, they argued, needed tranquillity to recover from the hurly-burly of urban living. Many people still find these kinds of principles helpful, substituting a trip to the Lake District with a walk to their allotment and some physical toil or a visit to a favourite green space to sit quietly and allow their senses some recovery time and space.

The softer function of exercise and movement

Finally, there is the softer function of exercise and movement. Something happens in your brain when you are exercising in certain rhythmically repetitive ways. Running, jogging or walking are good examples of this. Creative thoughts pop into the head – if not during the exercise then under the shower afterwards.

Either way, there is a creativity as well as a fitness gain. It seems that, when running, your mind finds its softer state where images and ideas that were not somehow consciously accessible can bubble up to the surface. For some people, dance can provide a similar effect, aided by the mood-enhancing properties of the music that often accompanies it. For others it is to activities like yoga that they turn to put their mind into its creatively relaxed state. Even if you have never tried yoga before, try this simple series of moves. They will only take five minutes and easily fit into a busy day.

NOW TRY THIS: **Yoga taster**

Try this simple exercise. Find a quiet spot in your home or garden. Take off your shoes and socks and make sure that you are in clothes that do not restrict your movement. Use the pictures and these instructions to help you do it. IN = inhale and EX = exhale. Try to breathe in and out slowly though your nose.

1. Stand with your arms by your sides and let your breathing settle.

2. As you breathe in, slowly raise your arms above your head. Then lower them as you breathe out. Do this four times.

3. Stand with your left leg forward and your right leg back. Raise your arms, as before, breathing in. This time, as you breathe out, lean forward, keeping your back as straight as possible. Let your hands touch the ground in front of your feet. Then breathe in as you bring your arms back up above your head and breathe out to bring them back down by your sides. Do this three more times. Then do it four times with your right leg forward and your left leg back. (Miss this one out if you have a bad back.)

4. Return to the standing position and let your breathing settle.

5. Now kneel on the floor and reach forward, putting your hands on the floor, like a cat stretching. As you breathe in, again like a cat, arch your back. Then let your back relax, breathe out and return to your forward stretch. Do this three more times.

6. Sit back on your haunches and let your breath settle.

Looking after your body

In 2001 a survey of 22,000 people in Britain for mynutrition.co.uk found:

76 per cent are often tired

58 per cent suffer from mood swings

52 per cent feel apathetic and unmotivated

50 per cent suffer from anxiety

47 per cent have difficulty sleeping.

Just a sign of the times in the developed world, you may be thinking. And you'd be partially right. These are tough times to be alive. Despite much scientific and technological progress, suicide is on the increase. More young people are suffering from mental health problems than ever before. What used to take us weeks to accomplish can be done in a trice nowadays and we are doubting our own abilities to keep up as a consequence. And we are all having to cope with food stuffed full of chemicals that were not even invented fifty years ago.

But you would also be largely wrong. It has always been like this. To get the best out of your mind and realize your creative potential, it has always been only too obvious that you need to look after your body. At this point it is tempting to invent a slightly moralizing voice telling us to drink more water, eat a more balanced diet, avoid alcohol, caffeine and chocolate, exercise more and generally become a contemporary ascetic. This is not the prescription we are offering you, although it is difficult to disagree with the sense of any of the items we have listed.

Rather, as with everything we have been describing so far, it is a case of being aware of complex relationships between what we do and how we see the world. Occasionally it may be better to have a few drinks, relax and wake up the next day feeling that a cloud has lifted than never indulge at all while remaining so stressed that you cannot get to sleep. Certainly it is essential that you stay in touch enough with your body to give your mind the best possible chance. Here is a very simple way of de-stressing your body and relaxing.

NOW TRY THIS: **Breathing with all your muscles**

Stand up, with your feet just slightly apart.

Take a deep breath in through your nose and then breathe out through your mouth. As you do so, place your hand on your stomach so that you can feel it moving up and down. Start to feel the difference between your midriff and your stomach. The goal is to feel as if your chest is already full of air before you actually start breathing.

Once you have established a regular pattern of breaths, start to focus on different parts of your body as you breathe. For each area, breathe in, tense the muscle group, count to five, then let it go loose as you breathe out. Then take three normal breaths in and out.

Start with your head. Clench all the muscles of your face, then relax them. Now move to your shoulders. Bring them up as close to your ears as possible. Then relax. Now do your arms, focusing on biceps and forearms. Then your hands.

Move on to stomach, lower back and bottom.

Then finally thighs, calves and feet.

How does that feel?

◾ Sleep on it

'The bed has become a place of luxury to me. I would not change it for all the thrones in the world.'

Napoleon Bonaparte

In today's fast-moving world there are more and more things to do each day and less and less time in which to do them. We work longer hours, watch more television and, with technological advances, can be on the telephone to someone the other side of the world twenty-four hours a day. The consequence of this is that most of us suffer from a lack of sleep.

We struggle by on six or seven hours, when seven or eight are what we need. All sorts of things are going on when we are asleep that will aid our creativity, as we began to see in Chapter 4 when we were looking at dreams. Memories from the preceding day are being laid down and stored. Chemicals are being produced which ensure that our body clock functions effectively. Sleep time is processing time for our mind. Have you ever experienced going to bed with a problem swirling around your head and waking up with the answer, not knowing how you came by it? This is a common enough occurrence for us to be respectful of the subtler benefits of sleeping.

NOW TRY THIS: Keeping a sleep and alertness diary

Keep a record of how alert you are feeling during a typical week.

Make a simple weekly diary, with 'wake up', 'early morning', 'morning', 'after lunch', 'late afternoon', 'evening' and 'late evening' marked on it.

Start each day by noting how many hours' sleep you had, including what time you went to bed and what time you got up. Make a note of whether you went to sleep and woke up when your body naturally wanted to, or because you had to. Then mark in the level of your alertness at different times of the day during the week.

At the end of the week study your diary carefully. When were you most and least alert? Which moods were most conducive to your creativity? What can you do to make sure you get more of these?

With sleeping as with waking, we are all different. We now have research evidence to support the feeling shared by many people that they are 'morning' or 'evening' people. One of the things you may want to investigate as a result of analyzing your sleep patterns is whether you are setting aside those periods of the day when you are at your most alert for those activities which demand the most creativity.

Creative people learn to go with the flow of their own bodily rhythms. For some the two hours before cock-crow may be their most fecund time, while others are just coming into their stride when the rest of their family are beginning to go to sleep.

■ You are what you eat

Diet matters for health. It also has a bearing on creativity. For your brain – so important an element of your creativity – is an enormous consumer of glucose and water. Deprive it of enough glucose or give it glucose in uneven doses, and concentration and memory tend to suffer. But while eating the right diet will undoubtedly help, it will not, sadly, make you into a creative genius.

A rough guide to staying healthy would include choosing complex carbohydrates and avoiding sugary foods. (Complex carbohydrates include things like whole grains, beans, nuts, fruit and vegetables. Complex carbohydrates are helpful because, unlike refined carbohydrates of the kind you get in sweets and sugary foods, they release glucose slowly rather than in quick bursts.)

In an age of increasing obesity, choosing the right kinds of fat is important. You need both saturated (omega 6) and unsaturated (omega 3) fat, but we tend to eat too much of the former. Omega 3 fat can be obtained most easily by eating fish, fish oils and certain kinds of seed oils such as flax, hemp and walnut. Many people choose to take fat supplements if they are unable to get enough in their regular diet for any reason. Eating lots of fresh fruit and vegetables is important. Proteins are essential for the production of amino acids called neurotransmitters in your brain. And water, of course, in good quantity, is necessary to keep you hydrated.

For many people, eating little and often is a good policy (we all know that full-stomach feeling and how lumpen it can make us feel, that is, if we have not dropped off to sleep.)

Much has been written about food and diet that is, frankly, contradictory and often not based on scientific fact. Patrick Holford's *Optimum Nutrition for the Mind* is a good reference book if you are hungry for more ideas.

■ Cultivating your aesthetic responses

Artist Betty Edwards recalls asking an art historian how he could tell, on viewing a painting by an unknown artist, whether it was any good. He replied: 'If my hands sweat, it's good.' We use physical words to describe the state in which our unconscious resonates with an experience, somehow recognizing its value, even its truth, without being able to explain. When we watch a good play we are 'touched'. When we read a poem that speaks to a deeper level in us, we are 'moved'.

The essence of the aesthetic response is to be moved, to have that feeling of 'rightness', but without being able to say why. The inner-net trembles and reverberates, but the habit map is lost for words. Argentinian writer Jorge Luis Borges said: 'Music, states of happiness, mythology, faces belaboured by time, certain twilights and certain places try to tell us something, or have said something we missed, or are about to say something: this imminence of a revelation which does not occur is, perhaps, the aesthetic phenomenon.'

Beauty is not a property of objects, or of nature, but of a certain kind of aesthetic response: one that hints to us that a good idea, something that is true to the deeper layers of our experience, is round the corner. For the artist, it may be sufficient, or perhaps even necessary, to create the hint and leave it at that. For the scientist or the manager, the aesthetic response may be the signal that a trail has been uncovered which will eventually, after a good deal of further work, lead to a novel theory or a profitable invention.

Being creative, therefore, involves learning to notice and value that aesthetic response. Cultivating this sensitivity is smart, even – maybe especially – for people who make a living out of coming up with good ideas in busy, complicated environments. They need their well-ordered prose; but perhaps schools of business administration should also be offering courses in 'creative writing' and 'the poetic sensibility'. Managers, as we have seen, have to be able to tolerate uncertainty and not-knowing. But more than this, they need to be able to enjoy it; to cultivate a feeling for the numinous possibility that may be strung through that confusion like a bright thread, capable of leading somewhere quite new.

Poetry is particularly good for inducing this kind of intuition. Poetry, at least of a certain kind, gets us used to this state of dwelling in something that both invites our interest and frustrates our understanding. It plays chords on the delicate strings of the inner-net, in such a way that we cannot reduce its reverberations to familiar tunes and categories. Paul Valéry described a poem as 'a kind of machine for inducing the poetic state of mind by means of words'. Coleridge said of poetry that it 'speaks most powerfully when it is generally, but not perfectly, understood'.

Even something as whimsical as Lewis Carroll's *Jabberwocky* leaves us with a feeling that is very different from having read a list of nonsense syllables, although that's what we've just done.

Twas brillig and the slithy toves
Did gyre and gimble in the wabe;
All mimsy were the borogroves,
And the mome raths outgrabe.

Alice, in the paragraph that follows the poem, puts her finger on its charm. 'It seems to fill my head with ideas – only I don't know exactly what they are,' she said. Sadly, many people have rejected the practice of reading and writing poetry, perhaps because of poor experiences at school and busy lifestyles dominated by television and computers.

NOW TRY THIS: Making a poem

Sit down with a pen and paper by you. First take time to relax, clear your mind and quieten your body. Now transport yourself to the lake by the dream house you created on page 84.

Sit by the side of the lake, gazing calmly across its tranquil surface. Feel the submerged life of the lake; all kinds of life forms cruising around out of sight. This lake is your unconscious. Feel how full it is, even though you can see nothing of what is in it.

Now choose a specific person, scenario or predicament with which you are having some unresolved difficulty at the moment and bring this issue into your consciousness. See if you can resonate with this predicament until you find something – a word, a phrase, an image, a face – that symbolizes it. Now toss the symbol into the middle of the lake and let it float there. Wait, quiet but alert. See what association comes up to the surface first. Don't think: let any association come.

Slowly open your eyes and write down a short phrase or sentence on your paper that describes this first 'fish' that you have caught. Now close your eyes and go back to the lake. Watch the floating symbol, and see what comes next. Don't free associate to the previous 'fish': keep going back to the symbol of your predicament. When you get your next 'bite' – maybe a memory or a fantasy this time – again write down a few words that help you capture it. Go back to the lake and do it again. Keep going until you have got about eight or ten lines, or until you have had no more 'bites' for at least a couple of minutes. Don't worry if the lines make no sense.

Open your eyes. Congratulations: you have written a 'poem' about your predicament. Leave it for now, and come back to your poem later. Mull it over quietly. See if it tells you anything.

This is how the poet Ted Hughes sometimes used to start a poem. He would place a central symbol of the poem at the centre of a page, and then generate round it a widening circle of associations and images thrown up by his unconscious. These could spread outwards and interconnect till the page as a whole looked like a mandala, or a diagram of a complicated molecule. When the page was full, it was time for Hughes to move on to a first draft proper, incorporating maybe only half of all the material he had generated.

To conclude this chapter, and bring the book to a close, here is part of a poem by Gillian Clarke about Ted Hughes and his use of this 'fishing' technique. With a soft-focus mind and lots of fishing practice we are confident that you will be able to hook the many ideas that are swimming around within your inner-net and safely land them on the shore of your mind.

... On the shore of the white page
the fisherman waits. His line is cast.
The house is quiet. Under its thatch
it is used to listening. It's all ears
for the singing line out-reeled from his touch
till the word rises with its fin of fire.
A tremor in the voice betrays a hand
held tense above the surface of that river,
patient at the deep waters of the mind
for a haul of dangerous silver.

■ Looking forward

The message of *The Creative Thinking Plan* is a simple one. Certain kinds of technique can help, but they are no substitute for gaining a much more fundamental understanding of the creative process. We have described some of the essential steps than you can take to stimulate your natural creativity. You can cultivate habits of mind which help, just as you can learn to influence your state of mind. Indeed, by becoming more aware of its three different dimensions, you can learn how to move between them, adopting the one most suited to the challenge you are facing. And you can also influence the environment around you while all the while ensuring that you stay healthy and in touch with yourself.

Index of 'Now Try This' exercises

Further reading

Adams, James, *Conceptual Blockbusting: a guide to better ideas.* Penguin 1987

Amabile, Teresa, *Creativity in Context.* Westview Press 1996

Cialdini, Robert, *Influence: science and practice.* Allyn and Bacon 2001

Claxton, Guy, *Hare Brain, Tortoise Mind.* Fourth Estate 1997

Claxton, Guy, *The Wayward Mind: an intimate history of the unconscious.* Little Brown, 2005

Csikszentmihalyi, Mihali, *Creativity: flow and the psychology of discovery and invention.* Harper Perennial 1996

Gelb, Michael, *How to Think Like Leonardo da Vinci.* Thorsons 1998

Gladwell, Malcolm, *The Tipping Point: how little things can make a big difference.* Little, Brown and Co. 2000

Grant, John, *After Image: mind-altering marketing.* Harper Collins 2002

Handy, Charles, *The Elephant and the Flea.* Random House 2002

Holford, Patrick, *Optimum Nutrition for the Mind.* Piatkus 2003

Hogarth, Robin, *Educating Intuition.* University of Chicago Press 2001

Howkins, John, *The Creative Economy: how people make money from ideas.* Penguin 2001

John-Steiner, Vera, *Notebooks of the Mind: explorations in thinking.* Oxford University Press 1997

Kao, John, *Jamming: the art and discipline of business creativity.* HarperCollinsBusiness 1997.

Koestler, Arthur, *The Act of Creation.* Dell 1964.

Langer, Ellen, *The Power of Mindful Learning.* Addison-Wesley 1997.

Lucas, Bill, *Power up Your Mind: learn faster, work smarter*. Nicholas Brealey 2001

Lucas, Bill, *Happy Families: how to make one, how to keep one*, BBC Active, 2006

Lucas, Bill, *Boost Your Mind Power Week by Week*, Duncan Baird, 2006

Osborn, Alex, *Applied Imagination*. CEF Press 1999

Pert, Candace, *Molecules of Emotion: why you feel the way you feel*. Simon and Schuster 1997

Plsek, Paul, *Creativity, Innovation and Quality*. ASQ Quality Press 1997

Robinson, Ken, *Out of Our Minds: learning to be creative*. Capstone 2001

VanGundy, Arthur, *Idea Power: techniques and resources to unleash the creativity in your organization*. Amacom 1992

What if?, *Sticky Wisdom: how to start a creative revolution at work*. Capstone 2002

Whyte, David, *The Heart Aroused: poetry and the preservation of the soul at work*. Industrial Society 1994

Picture acknowledgements

Page 62: © 2004 Magic Eye Inc.

Page 65: K. M. Dallenbach, 'A puzzle-picture with a new principle of concealment', *American Journal of Psychology*, 1951, vol. 64, 431–3.

Page 66: Sandro Del-Prete, www.illusoria.com

Drawings by Alan Burton unless credited above. The images on page 57 are drawn after Carmichael, Hogan and Walter.

Every effort has been made to trace copyright holders. Any who have not been contacted are invited to get in touch with the publishers.